ACCRINGTON HEYDAY

HERITAGE PUBLICATIONS, BLACKBURN, 2012

This book is copyright of Heritage Publications. Any unauthorised reprint or use of this material is prohibited. No part of this book may be reproduced or transmitted in any form or by any means, electronic or mechanical, including photocopying, without express permission from the publisher.

ISBN: 978-0-9572604-8-1

WWW.HERITAGEPUBLICATIONS.CO.UK

1878-1928.

THE JUBILEE SOUVENIR
OF THE
Corporation of Accrington.

Incorporated 15th February, 1878.

EDITED BY JOHN W. SINGLETON,
Fellow and Member of the Council of the Library
Association.
Lecturer in Librarianship at the University of Manchester.
BOROUGH LIBRARIAN

DEDICATED to the men and women of the
past who laid the foundations of the town
upon Industry and Progress, and to those with
vision of the future who realize the vast possibilities
of a greater Accrington.

FOREWORD.

IT is with pleasure I recommend a perusal of this Jubilee Souvenir to the consideration of our townspeople. Two objects have predominated in issuing it. *First,* that it may bring pleasant recollections of happy days to the memory of some of our older citizens. *Secondly,* that a recital of the town's municipal activities and of their growth during the past century, may inspire more of our younger citizens to devote some of their energies to the task of town-building. The process of decentralization is making the study of civics more and more important. That this Souvenir of our first fifty years as a municipality may realize these objects, and be valued in years to come as an interesting reminder of an outstanding epoch in the life of our town, is my sincere desire.

Mayor.

PREFACE.

THE primary purpose of this Jubilee Souvenir must be to record the town's progress municipally, but, in order to render the circle of its history complete it has been thought advisable to outline its earlier development and to illustrate its past.

I am indebted, not only to the authors of the several works named in the bibliography, but also to my friends Mr. Richard Ainsworth chiefly (but not solely), for the Section "The Birth of Modern Accrington"; Mr. Albert Hanson, for his ready help in securing illustrations; and Mr. John Ranson, A.M.I.M.E., F.G.S., for contributing the article on the Geology of Accrington and District. Also, to many chief officials for information concerning their departments, and to the members of the Library staff. Much of the labour of securing illustrations has been eased by the use it has been possible to make of the illustrations at Oak Hill Museum, largely due to the munificence of "Accrington Friend and Well-wisher." I also acknowledge the assistance of many helpers in securing other illustrations and portraits reproduced, and, not less, to some in their unsuccessful efforts to secure other portraits. Thanks are tendered to the owners of the copyrights for permission to reproduce them. The publication of this record, imperfect as it is, would have been much less complete without the help recorded.

One of the most important pieces of work on Accrington's early history is the Rev. W. H. Burgess's Notes published in the "Observer and Times," and it seems a pity they are not in some more permanent and accessible form. Is it too much to hope that the Corporation will, some day, have this basis of Accrington's history extended to date, print a complete history of the town, and include a bibliography of the known literature relating to it? It is too much to expect this to be undertaken by any individual as a speculation, though, with the increasing interest in local history, it might be made a financial success. The passing of each year makes the project more difficult and desirable.

J.W.S

CONTENTS.

Early Days	17
The Birth of Modern Accrington, by R. Ainsworth	29
The Old Lighting and Watching Days	59
Local Board of Health Days	63
Incorporation	85
Town Clerk's Department	95
Highways	99
Public Street Improvements and Development	103
Housing	109
Allotments	111
Health	111
The Police	117
Education	121
The Public Library	135
Electrical Engineering Department	141
Tramways	147
Public Cleansing	153
Cemetery	157
Markets	160
Weights and Measures	161
The Town Hall	162
Fire Brigade and Lighting	162
Parks	163
The Museum	171
The Public Baths	175
Abattoirs	177
Stables	177
General Finance	178
Accrington and District Gas and Water Supply	180
Sewerage and Sewage Disposal	185
The Geology of Accrington and District, by John Ranson, A.M.I.M.E., F.G.S.	191
Some Social and National Events of the Fifty Years	213
Mayors of the Borough, 1878-1928	219
Members of the Town Council, 1928	221
Miscellanea	223
Bibliography	225

LIST OF ILLUSTRATIONS.

Altham Church	19
Sketch of Black Abbey	19
High Riley Cottages	21
Broad Oak Fold	23
Higher Antley Hall	24
Lower Antley Hall	25
Gallows Hall	25
Slatepits Farm	26
Dunnyshop	26
Spire Farm	27
Bedlam	27
St. James's Church	29
Black Abbey Street	30
The Old Parsonage	31
John Hacking's Memorial Stone	32
Peel Fold, Oswaldtwistle	33
Hargreaves was given a hammer with which to smash his own machine	33
Broad Oak House	34
Sketch of Broad Oak Works (1814)	35
Manchester Road in more recent times	37
Rules and Orders of Friendly Society of Women (Title-page)	39
Union Street Cottages, 1787	40
Old King's Highway	41
The bottom of Manchester Road	44
The Old Round-about	44
Bank Brewery	45
View of Accrington, about 1848	46
Bull Bridge, formerly known as "Black Bull Bridge"	48
Accrington House	49
Hyndburn House	51
Lodge Cottage for Hyndburn House, Blackburn Road	51
Last Cattle Fair, Abbey Street	52
The Old Post Office	52
Old Shop in Abbey Street	53

Holden's Shop, Demolished, 1891	54
Pitt Entry, Abbey Street	55
View of Accrington in 1848	56
Briggs Yard, Abbey Street	57
The Old Pump, Pennyhouse	68
Certificate of Election of the First Local Board of Health	71
The Old Court House	73
Mr. Jas. Grimshaw	74
Mr. Swain Rhodes	76
Mr. William Dewhurst	76
Mr. Jas. Barlow	77
Site of the Market Hall	78
The Market Hall	79
Mr. Samuel Dugdale	80
Rev. John Rogers	81
Rev. Charles Williams	81
Mr. George W. Barlow	81
Mr. William Green	83
The Charter of Incorporation	87
Alderman John E. Lightfoot, First Mayor of Accrington	88
Town Council in 1880	89
Alderman T. E. Higham, Jubilee Mayor	90
Mrs. T. E. Higham, Jubilee Mayoress	90
Group of Mayors, 1878 to 1928 (with key)	91
The Town Council, 1928	92
The Corporation Officials, 1928	93
Mr. A. H. Aitken, Town Clerk, 1885-1926	95
Mr. W. H. Warhurst, Present Town Clerk	95
Mr. W. J. Newton, Borough Surveyor, 1888-1928	100
Grange Lane	102
Higher Grange Lane	104
Corner of Blackburn Road: Site of Bridge's Shop	105
Piccadilly before alterations	105
Corner of Blackburn Road and Abbey Street	106
The Old Black Dog Inn	106
Queen's Road before Development	107
Queen's Road to-day	108
Laneside Housing Scheme	110
Maternity Home, Rough Lee	115

National School, Church Street	121
Infant Street School	122
School Court, Church Street	124
Interior of Haywood's School	125
James Fenwick, School	127
Attendance Officer Mechanics' Institution and Willow House	130
The Grammar School, and the four Council Schools	131
The Public Library	138
Page from an Old Mill Record of 1792-3	140
Electricity Showrooms	146
Old Stearn Trams in Peel Street	148
Machpelah	158
The Town Hall	162
Milnshaw Park	164
Oak Hill Park	165
Oak Hill Park	165
Opening of Oak Hill Park	166
Hillock Farm	167
Bullough Park and Priestley Clough	167
Haworth Art Gallery	169
The War Memorial	172
The Museum	174
The Public Baths (interior)	176
Terminal Curvature in Haslingden Flags, Close Brow Quarry, Rishton	193
Glacial Conglomerate in River Calder	195
Great Arc Sandstone, Warmden Clough	201
Millstones in Lower Millstone Grits, Whalley Banks	204
The Victoria Hospital	213
Soup Kitchen, Infant Street School, 1895	215
The New Post Office, 1922	216

PLANS.

Peel Estate Plan, 1800	43
Centre of Accrington, 1849	66
Centre of Accrington, 1928	67

ILLUSTRATIONS.

Indebtedness is expressed to the owners of the copyright of the many illustrations used, including:

Councillor R. I. Constantine, Mr. C. F. Dawson, Alderman G. H. Ellis, Mr. W. Fielding, Mr. A. Greenwood, Mr. H. S. Grimshaw, Mr. A. Hanson, Mr. R. Harrison, Mrs. Harvey, Mr. C. Haworth, Messrs. Hepworth & Webster, Mr. H. M. Jones, Mr. B. Leaver, Messrs. Moffitt Bros., Mr. J. Ranson, Mr. C. E. Riley, Messrs. Tattersall, Mr. J. A. Walmsley, Mr. T. Walton, Mr. J. Watson, Mr. T. Woods.

EARLY DAYS.

IT is quite a natural thing for an inhabitant of a district to set his mind wondering upon its condition in past ages. What it looked like. What sort of people trod its cloughs, fields, and hills before him. How it was governed and who were its "big men." Such questions arise naturally at definite epochs in the life of a municipality such as a Jubilee of Incorporation, which Accrington celebrates in this year of grace, one thousand nine hundred and twenty-eight.

Chroniclers of Accrington's past, and they are more numerous than is generally supposed, have not unearthed any specific reference to its existence earlier than about the beginning of the 12th century, but, that the district was peopled in much earlier times sufficient proof is at hand. Its very name has a Saxon ring about it and, despite the lure of the "Oak," with its appeal to Englishmen, we lean to the view expressed by Mr. Burgess that Accrington was, in Saxon times, "Akeringa's town." This writer says: "Many Saxon patronymics, or family and tribal names, had the termination 'inga,' and the place of settlement was their tun, or ton or town. Accrington is the Akeringa's town." Custom dies hard, and many of the older Accringtonians still pronounce the name as if it was intended to be divided into four syllables, not three Ak-ker-ing-ton. The Rev. Charles Williams inclines to the Saxon origin, but interprets the meaning of Akerington as the "Oak-field enclosure."

But was there no earlier settlement of people in the district than those of Akeringa's days? Until quite recent years it had been assumed by the generally recognized "authorities" on palceolithic research that the presence of ice and the absence of flint were the insuperable barriers to the existence (and subsistence) of prehistoric man in Northern England. It was so eminent an authority as Sir John Evans who first cast some doubt upon this hypothesis, indicating that other factors entered into the consideration of the case: that other material than flint might have been used, and that the assumed absence of palceolithic implements in the north of England might be due to their not having been found and not to their non-existence. It is to the credit of Dr. T. E. Nuttall that local interest in the existence of prehistoric man in these parts has been aroused. Acting upon the suggestion that if prehistoric man inhabited these parts his tools would be manufactured from material other than flint, Dr. Nuttall searched the banks of the old streams, and at length discovered what he is convinced is a palceolithic "floor." Many stone implements of recognized shape, bearing evidences of fabrication, have been found, and, whatever may be the view as to their authenticity (and it must be admitted some are sceptical) the fact of so many implements being found together, within a few yards of each other, is a difficult one to overcome. It certainly points to design rather than accident. Indeed, if Dr. Nuttall's view is not correct, a miracle must have occurred in order to bring together so closely the evidences of the existence of prehistoric man within an hour's easy walk from the centre of Accrington.

If, therefore, you do cast your mind's eye back in a vision of the early inhabitants of this district, let it travel far enough back to the days when early man trod the turf in search of food, bearing a murderous looking, and, of its type, extremely effective stone weapon.

But whilst these evidences may be considered vague, and by some unreliable, there are more tangible evidences of Saxon occupancy and absolute proof of the existence of Akerington, as witnessed in a charter by which Henry de Lacy granted Elvetham (Altham), Clayton, and Akerington to Hugh, son of Leofwine (founder of Altham Church, circa 1140), about the middle of the twelfth century. This was the beginning of its history in reliable record. Its next notable event was a distressing one to the inhabitants.

ALTHAM CHURCH.

SKETCH OF BLACK ABBEY.

Accrington was detached from Altham, and given to the Abbot and monks of Kirkstall, by Robert de Lacy, about the year 1200, and in their hands it remained for some 80 to 90 years. The new owners did not treat the inhabitants with the consideration one might have expected from a religious body, but dispossessed them of their dwellings and built a grange, or farmstead. This autocratic treatment was deeply resented by the early inhabitants of our town and they took the law into their own hands, burnt the grange and murdered the three lay brothers in charge of it. The Abbot appealed to his patron, Robert de Lacy, who meted out punishment in true thirteenth century manner, and "peace was restored." The Abbot of Kirkstall, towards the end of the thirteenth century, found himself in some financial difficulty, and was willing for a consideration in money to be relieved of his Accrington estate, and it reverted to the De Lacy family, then Earls of Lincoln. To this Ecclesiastical ownership we owe the place names of "The Grange," "Black Abbey," and "Abbey Street."

In the third edition of Whitaker's "History of Whalley" (1818), reference is made to the sale of the Chapel of Accrington with one bell, to the inhabitants, for the sum of 46s. 8d., and the historian continues "A little above the Chapel is a house called the Grange, and still nearer another, which yet bears the name of The Black Abbey. This has been rebuilt within memory. but I have no doubt that here was the cell of the monks of Kirkstall at Accrington." These ruins occupied the site of Oak Street Congregational School, prior to 1840. On the reversion of the estates, the Earl appointed a steward to control them, and from his records it appears that whilst £13 2s. 11¾ d. (including arrears of £2 13s. 7¾d.), was received in the year 1295-6, the expenses were £11 2s. 4½d., leaving the owner but £2 0s. 7¼d. Robert Rylay (Riley) presented these accounts as steward on behalf of his lord. High Riley Cottages are closely associated with the history of Accrington, and were the home of the Riley family for over five hundred years. The present building (which has been converted into cottages), was erected in 1628, and is the oldest dated building in the town. The rolls containing the De Lacy accounts are preserved in the Public Record Office: they may also be seen in volume 112 of the Transactions of the Chetham Society at the library.

It is not the purpose of this volume to give more than a very brief outline of Accrington's progress to its present position. Its history has, to a large extent, already been written. To follow the history of any town closely requires very careful study: sources of study are suggested in the bibliography accompanying this volume. Its inhabitants gradually expanded the borders of the clearing. It would be a constant warfare with wild animals, wolves particularly, and the hardly less wild human beings. In days when "the forester" had almost unlimited authority, and the life of a human being was reckoned at much less than that of a deer, existence must have been a struggle. The land gradually became more cultivated, less of scrub and forest, the haunt of the deer, and more of arable and pasture land, the mark of cultivation. In the beginning of the sixteenth century the struggle was with high powers, the tenants who had been granted leases and effected considerable "improvements" fought for the confirmation and establishment of the copyhold estates. Mr. James Broughton says (1910): "After much agitation and litigation in which the Cunliffes, of Hollins, took a leading part, the cultivated waste lands became by Act of Parliament, the Manor of Accrington New Hold in the year 1507, and are, to this day, held as customary Copyholds." (Copyhold tenure was abolished by the Law of Property Act, 1922. Ed.)

HIGHER RILEY COTTAGES.

They did not hold the right they gained without further struggle, for in the early years of the seventeenth century we find them mulcted in "fines" to the King for land they had reclaimed, or faced with the alternative of being turned out of their holdings.

Accrington, of course, did not escape the turmoil of the Civil War: the most noticeable participants in the struggle being Nicholas Cunliffe, of Hollins, and Robert Cunliffe, of Sparth (Clayton-le-Moors). Both were on the side of the Parliamentarians, and took an active part in the struggles to free Lancashire from the Royalist forces. Wars, civil and otherwise, as we have found to our cost, are expensive procedures, and one of the most interesting documents relating to the history of our town was the Act passed, upon the Restoration, for raising money to payoff the soldiers and naval forces. This, in effect, was an income tax, everyone above 16 years of age was called upon to pay in proportion to his estate. The names are of interest Kenion, Cunliffe, Worsley, Hargreaves, Haworth, Riley, Clayton, Grymshaw, Rishton, Walmsley, Pilkington, Holden. The trades Clothier, Waller, Butcher, Webster (weaver), Wright, Gunsmith, Ale-house keeper, Husbandman, Labourer, Joiner, Slater. The amount received from Accrington was £19 16s. 1d.

The town's history from now to the Birth of Modern Accrington, when it became one of the important centres of the calico printing industry, is centred chiefly around its family dwellings.

BROAD OAK FOLD. The grouping of dwellings in folds was for protective purposes. This particular one received its name from the presence in its midst of a huge old oak tree, blown down in the great gale of 1817. It was the home of the Walmsley family for generations, and later of the Halsteads and Taylors.

HIGHER ANTLEY HALL is an interesting old seventeenth century dwelling, its chief archaeological interest being the mullioned windows, blocked up with stone in evasion of the exceedingly unpopular window tax. Since 1735, it has, until recently, been part of the endowment of St. James's Church.

LOWER ANTLEY HALL, built about the beginning of the seventeenth century, was one of the most ancient halls in Accrington, and was situated where Lonsdale Street and Newark Street now stand. The Rishtons inhabited it until 1821. In later years it was divided into tenements, and was finally demolished to make way for town improvements.

GALLOWS HALL, until quite recently the Club House of the Baxenden Golf Club, consisted formerly of two cottages erected in the eighteenth century. The name has a sinister meaning in all probability associated with the killing and stealing of deer in the surrounding forest and its attendant punishment.

SLATE PITS FARM. The earliest portion of the building is of the seventeenth century. Once part of the Riley estate, it was for many years the home of a branch of the Hacking family, but reverted to the Rileys.

DUNNYSHOP (Dunschopfal) was built in the sixteenth century. It is now used as a farm, but was originally the residence of a branch of the Rishtons.

BROAD OAK FOLD.

HIGHER ANTLEY HALL.

SPIRE FARM, or, New High Riley. A conspicuous landmark to the east of Accrington. The prominent feature is the castellated tower which formerly was a portion of Old High Riley.

GREEN HAWORTH, though part of the borough hardly seems of it. It still retains its eighteenth and early nineteenth century appearance, though the housing scheme in Willows Lane has brought it a little nearer to the activities of the town. It is difficult to account for the portion named "Bedlam," but references to this are to be found as early as the twelfth century.

The life of the community, so far as known records shew, was somewhat humdrum, but there is evidence of movement towards a larger field of influence in the later days of the eighteenth century, and from then onwards the sources of information are considerable.

LOWER ANTLEY HALL.

GALLOWS HALL.

SLATEPITS FARM.

DUNNYSHOP.

SPIRE FARM.

BEDLAM.

THE BIRTH OF MODERN ACCRINGTON.
By R. Ainsworth.

THE eighteenth century, for the most part, was a slumbering time for Accrington, undisturbed by stirring events in other parts of Lancashire. The old Wardens' Book, preserved at St. James's Church, is the record of Accrington's local government during that period. A list of the Posts indicates the system of appointing Chapel Wardens, while the list of overseers for Old Accrington is complete from 1681 to 1774. From Bishop Gastrell's Visitation we have information regarding a school founded in 1716, and evidence of its existence can be traced by legacies until 1749.

Renewed interest in religious affairs is shown by the building of the present St. James's Church in 1763, replacing the old chapel of 1546. The Baptists opened Machpelah Chapel in Hyndburn Road, in 1765, and the Methodists commenced in the Lower Fold, in 1788.

ST JAMES'S CHURCH.

Associated with the church life of the late eighteenth and early nineteenth centuries, are the two old houses in Black Abbey Street with round-headed doorways, one of which was occupied by the

Rev. John Hopwood, when he came to Accrington in 1812. Three years later he removed to the Old Parsonage, Heifer Bank, which was the residence of the clergy until 1856. But a great industrial change was at hand.

INDUSTRIAL DEVELOPMENT.
The woollen industry was well established in the district, when the woollen yarn was spun by the women folk of the household with the aid of the distaff and spinning wheel, the handloom being an accessory in almost every home.

BLACK ABBEY STREET.

The introduction of cotton furnished the material for a cheaper and more convenient fabric, which gradually displaced the ancient industry in Lancashire. The cotton had to be spun upon the same implements as wool, and the handloom weavers were often at a standstill for want of yarn. With these hindrances the demand for cotton goods increased far beyond the power of supply, and the value of the goods was greatly enhanced. This state of things acted as a stimulus for enterprise and invention, and Lancashire was in the forefront in this respect. With Kay, Arkwright, and Crompton, are to be added the local names, James Hargreaves of Stanhill, inventor of the spinning jenny, and John Hacking of Huncoat, of whom there is a memorial at Altham. He invented a carding engine, turned by hand, and carded cotton wool for his neighbours, in 1772.

THE OLD PARSONAGE.

JOHN HACKING'S MEMORIAL STONE.

The first evidence of the industrial development in Accrington, is afforded by a record of 1780, when there were five small spinning mills employing a total of forty persons; thus was born the local factory system.

At Peel Fold, Oswaldtwistle, Robert Peel experimented in calico printing, which had been introduced into Lancashire at Bamber Bridge, in 1764. It was due to Robert Peel and his sons, that calico printing was so well established in North-East Lancashire; the pioneer works in the district, being Brookside, Oswaldtwistle, in which had also been installed the spinning jennies of Hargreaves.

PEEL FOLD, OSWALDTWISTLE.

HARGREAVES WAS GIVEN A HAMMER WITH WHICH TO SMASH HIS OWN MACHINE.

The first of the riots directed against the introduction of machinery occurred in 1779, which resulted in Hargreaves, of Stanhill, having his machines destroyed, and himself leaving the district. After this, Church Works was founded by the Peels, which became the chief centre from which originated numerous other printworks, such as Foxhill Bank and Oakenshaw.

The influence of the Peels induced three local men Fort, Taylor, and Bury, to found Broad Oak Printworks in 1782, from which can be dated practically the modern industrial development of Accrington. It was the chief line of industry for a long period, and brought about a decided increase in the local population. Benjamin Hargreaves, in his "Recollections of Broad Oak and Description of the Printworks," gives an interesting account of its subsequent development. Broad Oak House was built by John Hargreaves of Broad Oak Printworks, who also built the "New Factory," in 1834. The illustration shews the house before it was demolished and rebuilt by the late Sir George W. Macalpine.

BROAD OAK HOUSE.

The first recorded strike in Accrington occurred in 1815. At that time the masters had to pay an excise duty of threepence per yard of cloth printed for home trade. They claimed that they could not pay the charge and the high rate of wages to the blockprinters, and proposed a reduction of wages. A strike ensued, which extended throughout the calico printing trade in North-East Lancashire. The foreman blockprinter was fired at in Shop Lane, leading to Broad Oak, but escaped unhurt, a reward of £50 was offered for the arrest of the man who had discharged the weapon: a copy of this poster is in Oak Hill Museum.

Thomas Hargreaves, the founder of the Hargreaves family of Broad Oak, Accrington, was born at Wheatley Lane, Pendle Forest. He was engaged in the calico business at Sabden, where he became manager, and later came to Broad Oak.

SKETCH OF BROAD OAK WORKS (1814).

On the dissolution of the partnership, Mr. Fort retained Oakenshaw and Mr. Bury, Sabden Works, while Mr. Thomas Hargreaves became partner with Mr. Adam Dugdale of Broad Oak Works (1811). Under the direction of Thomas Hargreaves, Broad Oak flourished, and extensive alterations were carried out at the works, which, by 1814 (at which date the illustration gives the extent), had been completed; including the arching over the river for some distance. Broad Oak in 1814 as shewn here is from an old sketch, and illustrates the extent of the works at that time. The four-storey building, formerly known as the old bell shop, had then only just been erected. The print may not be correct in its delineation of the neighbourhood, but is useful for comparative purposes. The valuation of Broad Oak Printworks, July 1st, 1822, placed at £253 16s. 8d., is an interesting document.

1790 SURVEY.
A survey of the township of New Accrington for 1790, signed by James Walmsley and Peter Sefton, is the earliest known for Accrington, and is now in the Public Reference Library.

Area of township, 1,448 acres, 1 rood and 24 perches. Yearly Value, £1,510 15s. 3¼d. Rates, £17 6s. 7¾d. The rate on land was 3d. in the £. The rate on cottages, 2d. in the £. Included in the survey are: three Carding Engines; two Dyehouses; one Fulling Mill; one Loom House; one Pencilling Shop.

The Badge Book of Henry Ratcliffe, now in Oak Hill Museum, is of interest as giving food prices, etc., from 1789 to 1792. Among the items are: Butter = 5½d. per lb.; Best Meal = 10½d. per 3-lbs.; Flour = 3/7 ½d. per 17-lbs.; Bread = 3½d. per loaf; Beef-4½d. per lb.; Breast = 4d. per lb.; Candles = 7½d. per lb.; Tobacco = 2½d. per ounce; Cottage Rent = 6d. per week.

By 1801 the population had grown to 3,077. As evidence of the importance of the calico printing industry at that time, of the 75 entries in the directory of Accrington for 1818, no less than 25 refer to people connected with it. The introduction says: "There are several very extensive printing works in this district. In 1811, Old Accrington contained 885 inhabitants and 180 houses, and New Accrington, 2,381 inhabitants and 425 houses."

MANCHESTER ROAD IN MORE RECENT TIMES, SHEWING
THE DEVELOPMENT OF BROAD OAK WORKS.

ACCRINGTON WORKHOUSE.

In 1797, the local vestry instructed the overseer to obtain plans for the erection of a workhouse for the relief of the poor of New Accrington, the expenses to be defrayed by the landowners and farmers of the township. The delayed project came into notice in August, 1799, owing to the distress caused by a tremendous storm of wind and rain which ruined the harvest.

On the 4th September, 1801, the townships of Old and New Accrington, Church, and Oswaldtwistle, agreed to amalgamate for poor-law purposes. From a minute in the records for 1803, the rates for interest on the money borrowed, £800, were thus apportioned: Old Accrington, £13 15s. 0d.; New Accrington, £28 15s. 6d. The Workhouse erected in Union Street was three stories high, "eight windows long," with a door at the north end, standing well back from the street, it was surrounded on all four sides with a strong stone wall, eight feet high, and two feet thick, an iron door was at the King Street corner. On July 26th, 1808, Thomas Mersey and his wife, from Hoghton, were appointed master and matron, at a salary of £25, together with tea and sugar. The minute recording the appointment has the following:

"If the man has not sufficient employment he is to work and the benefit is to go to the several townships."

"If his wife acts as midwife on any occasion, she is to receive four shillings, but she is not to exercise these functions out of the workhouse."

Here is an ingenious method of relieving the rates, but no minutes record to what extent Mr. Mersey was able to effect this by working outside the workhouse walls. This may be looked upon as the precursor of the Accrington Maternity Home.

In 1813, the Church Rate was consolidated with the Poor Rate, and in 1814, a visiting committee of gentry was appointed for the Workhouse. It was decided in 1817, to sell the workhouse, but it was not until 1824, that the Wesleyans purchased a portion for £117, and from that date until 1844, they continued to acquire further portions of the old Workhouse. When the whole site had been acquired, the Workhouse was demolished to make way for the School. In 1837, the Haslingden Union was formed, with one representative from Old Accrington and three from New Accrington.

Accrington was not behind hand in the general formation of Friendly Societies following upon the passing of Rose's Act, in 1793, which encouraged their formation not only by word, but by affording relief from taxation.

The earliest record of such a Friendly Society in Accrington, founded only a few years after the passing of the Act, is a book of Rules, Orders, and Regulations for a society of women, founded July 1st, 1799, at the house of Joseph Scholfield, the Rose and Crown Inn, New Accrington. The illustration is of the title-page of the book, which is the earliest printed record of Accrington. Printed at Blackburn, by R. Parker, Bookseller, Bookbinder, and Stationer, 1807. A list of the names of 63 members is added.

RULES, ORDERS,
AND
REGULATIONS,
TO BE OBSERVED FOR THE
GOVERNMENT AND GUIDANCE
OF A
SOCIETY OF WOMEN,
CALLED THE
Friendly Society of Women,
HELD AT THE HOUSE OF
JOHN SCHOLFIELD,
THE
ROSE and CROWN INN,
IN NEW ACCRINGTON,
IN THE
PARISH OF WHALLEY,
AND COUNTY OF LANCASTER.
Begun, the FIRST Day of July, in the Year of
our Lord, 1799.

Blackburn:
Printed by R. Parker, Bookseller, Bookbinder, and Stationer
1807.

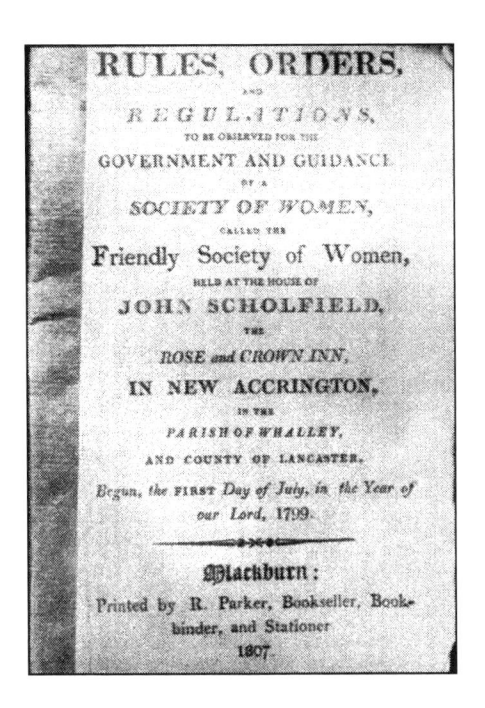

A Women's Friendly Society was founded at the George Inn (now Black Horse), Abbey Street, Accrington, on the 27th August, 1811. A book of rules, dated 1818, gives the name of the landlady (Alice Hall), at the head of the list of members.

These women's societies were numerous in Accrington district about this period. The annual club day was celebrated by a dinner and festivities, when the members vied with each other as to which had the finest cap, and prizes were awarded accordingly.

UNION STREET COTTAGES.

EARLY BUILDING SOCIETY.

As a result of the industrial development which took place, the population of Accrington began to increase, and cottage property to be erected. The first evidence of this was the building of Union Street, in 1787, so named from a building society, or union, of which early thrift society there does not appear to be any existing documentary record. Plantation Mill Square, Duncan Square, Oswaldtwistle, and Nelson Square, Church, were early building schemes in connection with the neighbouring printworks. Evidence of deeds proves the activity of building societies in the erection of property in Abbey Street, 1815, and Warner Street, in 1828. The earliest book of rules for such a society in the Reference Library is the following: Rules, and Regulations to be observed by the members of the Accrington Building and Investment Society, for building and purchasing dwelling houses, etc., established 19th January, 1837, at the Black Bull Inn, in Accrington. Accrington: printed, by R. J. Salter.

At a meeting held at the Black Bull Inn, in Old Accrington, on the fifteenth day of December, one-thousand-eight-hundred-and-thirty-six, it was agreed that the following rules and orders be adopted by the Society, and that 100 copies be printed for its use.

Then follow twenty rules governing the Society, the second rule stating that the meetings shall be held monthly, on the Thursday on or next before the full of the moon, at the Black Bull Inn, in Accrington aforesaid, or at the house of such publican member who shall hold the greatest number of shares in this Society.
A later similar society held meetings at Carter's Institute, an old building still existing behind Oak Street.

OLD KING'S HIGHWAY.

TURNPIKE ROADS.
Two estate maps comprising the Lee-Warner and Peel Lands, dated 1800, are the earliest known maps of Accrington, and are here reproduced. They are sufficient to indicate Accrington's extent at the close of the eighteenth century, which consisted of the two townships of Old and New Accrington: two hamlets principally centred around Bull Bridge and Lower Fold for Old Accrington, and around St. James's Church and Higher Fold for New Accrington. The old King's Highways Grange Lane and Hollins Lane, leading to Manchester, King Street and Willows Lane to Blackburn, Milnshaw

Lane to Whalley, Mill Gate and Penny House to Huncoat and Burnley, Sandy Lane to the King's Highway on Hameldon. The new Turnpike road is indicated as the new highway from Whalley to Manchester. The contract was let in 1789, and the road constructed 1790-91, by John Metcalf, known as Blind Jack-o'-Knaresboro', the last line of road he constructed before he retired in 1792 to Yorkshire.

The roads were under the control of the Turnpike Trusts, and Toll Gates were erected along the new roads with Bar Houses. The earliest Accrington Toll Bar is the Old Round-about, in Manchester Road; known originally as the Grange Bridge Bar. Its interest has, to a great extent, been destroyed by the substitution of modern panes of glass for the old rounded ones. This was displaced later by the Bar House near Oak Hill Park, the lower end of Hollins Lane being then chained to assist, hence the old cottages near by became known as the Chain-houses.

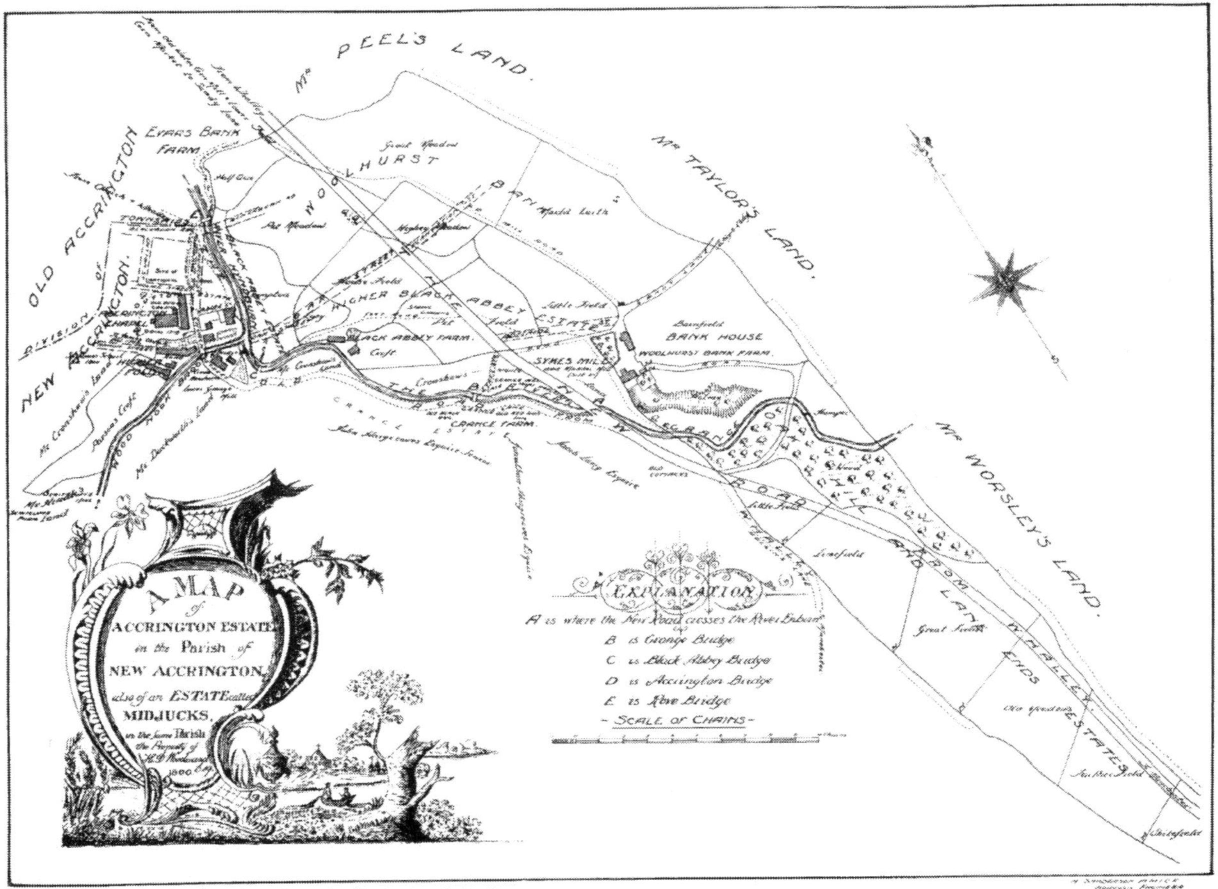

The lines of Blackburn Road, Oak Street, Plantation Street, etc., shown thus — — — have been inserted on this copy of Mr. Johnson's Plan of 1800 as a means of location

THE BOTTOM OF MANCHESTER ROAD, SHOWING
COMMENCEMENT OF NEW TURNPIKE ROAD.

THE OLD ROUND-ABOUT.

44

Benjamin Hargreaves, in his "Recollections of Broad Oak," states that business men used to collect at the Hare and Hounds Inn, Enfield, and travel on horseback together to Manchester for business. A change came over this mode of travelling in 1815, when the first stage coach from Clitheroe to Manchester passed through Accrington. This was regarded as a great innovation, until in 1848, there were seven coaches daily traversing Accrington. The Red Lion Hotel, in Abbey Street, was the principal coaching inn, the old buildings behind, formerly the old cowhouses farm, being the centre of activity for the changing of horses. Coaches also called at the Hargreaves Arms, Commercial, and Bay Horse, but only occasional ones, at the latter part of the period. Burnley Road was the last of the local turnpike roads to be constructed (1838). The original toll bar was opposite the present Boar's Head, later removed to the Accrington side of the Cemetery. One of the earliest buildings was Bank Brewery, still standing.

BANK BREWERY.

An outstanding enterprise in the development of Accrington was the coming of the railway, which was opened to Blackburn on June 19th; to Manchester, August 17th; and to Burnley, in September of the same year (1848).

The Leeds and Liverpool Canal was in the making at the same period as the roads, and was opened from Burnley to Enfield in 1796, but the entire length was not finished until 1816.

These two enterprises, affording ready means of transit, assisted materially in advancing the industrial development of Accrington.

VIEW OF ACCRINGTON ABOUT 1848, FROM AN OLD GUIDE TO THE EAST LANCASHIRE RAILWAY.

EARLY COTTON MILLS.
One of the early cotton mills in Accrington was that of Messrs. Pilling, in Grange Lane, the site of the present Royal Mill. The following advertisement appeared in the "Blackburn Mail":

"Machinery-
"To be sold by auction, on Thursday, the 31st day of October, 1805, at the Factory belonging to John Pilling, of Accrington, near Haslingden.
"Two Carding Engines, one Devil, one Drawing Frame, one double speed Slubbing Frame, twenty spindles; two Roving Frames,

forty spindles each; one Reel, four (Spinning) Mules, 210 spindles each; three new Throstles, 120 spindles each; a great number of Cans and Bobbins, with various other articles.

"Time of payment will be fixed on day of sale."

Grange Mill, familiarly known in later times as the Old Factory, situated at the corner of Syke Street and Grange Lane, was erected soon after 1821, by the Sykes family; here power looms were first introduced into Accrington.

RIOTS.
The "Gentleman's Magazine," for May, 1826, gives the following account of the power loom riots as they affected Accrington:
"On the 24th April, accounts were received from Accrington, and its vicinity, that a mob, consisting of several thousand men, had marched, some armed with pikes and others with bludgeons, and a part even with fire-arms, into the village, and proceeded to the factory of Messrs. Sykes. A party of the First Dragoon Guards, stationed at Blackburn, were immediately despatched, and they met the mob proceeding in the direction of Blackburn, but having no one competent to give the necessary orders, they were obliged to let them pass."

Benjamin Hargreaves relates how his brother Robert, witnessed the smashing of the machinery at Sykes' Mill, after having a mass meeting on Whinney Hill. At Sykes' Mill, 60 looms were destroyed; at Walmsley's, Rough Hey, 20; and at Westall's, White Ash, Oswaldtwistle, 80.

Owing to the distress caused by these industrial disturbances, the Government offered loans for public works. Mr. McAdam, a noted surveyor and improver of road construction, visited Blackburn, and there met the Rev. John Hopwood and Benjamin Hargreaves, a deputation appointed by a public meeting at Accrington, to suggest a new road to Blackburn. Ultimately the road was constructed in 1827, and handed over to the Bury and Whalley Trust commissioners.

The result of the riots also led to a company of military being stationed in Accrington. They were located in the old Workhouse in Union Street; previously, during the 1815 strike, the soldiers had been billeted in the five inns of the village.

In 1842, occurred the Plug Drawing Riots. An old Accrington tradesman's diary records:
"August 13th. Mob here, and stopped all the works.
"August 15th. Mob again here, pressed all in their way."

The inhabitants held a meeting and decided that such proceedings should be resisted if the mob came again; when 600 or 700 special constables were sworn in.

"August 19th. Constables exercising; regaled in Oak Field, expecting the mob."

BULL BRIDGE, FORMERLY KNOWN AS "BLACK BULL BRIDGE," NOW OCCUPIED BY THE AMBULANCE DRILL HALL.

ACCRINGTON HOUSE.

DEVELOPMENT OF ACCRINGTON.

In the early days of the nineteenth century, Accrington was a pretty rural village, clustered chiefly around the old centres of St. James's Church and Bull Bridge, with Abbey Street and Union Street representing the newer Accrington that owed its inception to the industrial revolution of the late eighteenth century.

Abbey Street owes its present irregular appearance to the original cottage property having gardens in front. Behind the street on the east towards the Coppice was Peel Park, in the midst of which stood Accrington House, the residence of Jonathan Peel (brother of the first Sir Robert Peel, who was born at Peel Fold). Accrington House, the largest mansion in the town at one period, was built by Jonathan Peel, in the latter part of the eighteenth century. Jonathan Peel was "the squire of the village," and an examination of records seems to prove that it was part of the squire's duty to head all subscription lists possibly it was *infra dig* for anyone to subscribe more than the squire. The park extended to the bottom of Avenue Parade. The house was demolished towards the end of 1889. Hyndburn House was re-built by Robert Peel, junior, in the park alongside Blackburn

Road, after that road was constructed, and later became the residence of Frederick Steiner. The Lodge Cottage stood where the Grammar School has been erected.

Abbey Street came into existence alongside the new highway, and became the principal thoroughfare of the village, and the Market Street, during the early coaching era; a market being established here in the early thirties. Later, a number of the cottages became converted into shops, an old time example being the one illustrated, and whose best known occupant was John Law. It was near Pitt Entry, which led to an old well. Another quaint old shop was that of Holden, the Clogger, at the corner of Blackburn Road and Abbey Street; it was occupied by that family for over 50 years.

In 1818, the post office was in Abbey Street, with James Cocker as Post Master, the mails in the early part of the century being carried on horseback, but later by the mail coaches. Accrington August Fair was established on the Bay Horse pavements in 1825, later extending up Warner Street into Abbey Street. The illustration shews the last cattle fair to be held in Abbey Street.

In 1831, the population was 6,283, housed in 1,206 dwellings. These had increased in 1841, to 8,719 and 1,666 respectively.

The rateable value increased from £24,829 in 1841 to £35,782 in 1861, when the population was 17,688, and the number of houses, 3,404.

HYNDBURN HOUSE.

LODGE COTTAGE FOR HYNDBURN HOUSE,
BLACKBURN ROAD.

THE OLD POST OFFICE.

LAST CATTLE FAIR, ABBEY STREET.

OLD SHOP IN ABBEY STREET.

HOLDEN'S SHOP, DEMOLISHED 1891.

PITT ENTRY, ABBEY STREET.

Accrington, during the first half of the nineteenth century, emerged from its village state to a town of 10,376 population, in 1851. The old mortality sheets give some idea of the death rate of the period. The view of Accrington, in 1848, gives an impression of the extent of the town at that time, with the districts of Peel Park and Hollins still rural and park lands. The directory of 1825, adds two more inns, and several more names of tradesmen beyond those recorded in 1818.

VIEW OF ACCRINGTON IN 1848.

1837 saw the erection of Broad Oak Mill, better known as the New Factory, which dates an era in the cotton industry of Accrington. Messrs. Howard and Bleakley, in 1853, commenced Globe Works; an event second only in importance to the founding of Broad Oak; in the industrial history of Accrington.

The Accrington Weavers Association had their early meeting place at Briggs Yard, Abbey Street, in the building illustrated, which also saw the beginnings of the local co-operative movement, in 1859.

BRIGGS YARD, ABBEY STREET.

A Botanical Society, 1847, was the predecessor of the Accrington Naturalists' and Antiquarian Society, founded July 22nd, 1855, which had at one time, a museum in Abbey Street.

Space forbids a more detailed account of this formative period of Accrington, when, from a small village with the primitive government of a Vestry meeting, one constable and magistrate as the executive authority for law and order, to a town prepared for self-government by way of lighting and watching inspectors and a Local Board. With the advent of the Local Board, Accrington was launched upon a successful career in municipal government.

THE OLD LIGHTING AND WATCHING DAYS.

IN the forties and early fifties, the Lighting and Watching Inspectors were the governing power in the town in addition to the Vestry: they were elected at a public meeting of ratepayers.

The earliest record of the public lighting of the town is to be found in the Minute Books of the meetings of the Inspectors: they are four in number, and form interesting reading. The first entry is of the 7th October, 1841, but there must be earlier records giving the date of the adoption of the sections of the act of King William IV, for the Lighting and Watching of Parishes. The entry of that date records an arrangement with the Accrington Gas Company, for the "necessary pillars, lamps, and lamp irons, properly fitted up," and for two thousand hours' lighting, at 55/- per year for each lamp. The arrangement was for three years, but if the profits of the Company exceeded five per cent. a reduction of 2/6 per lamp per annum was to be allowed. Mr. Harrison says: "The first Contract with the Gas and Water Company for lighting with gas the public lamps within the township of Old Accrington, was for the sum of two pounds ten shillings per lamp per annum, the lamps to be lit half an hour after sunset to one hour before sunrise"; this was dated August 11th, 1843, so it would appear that the resolution of October, 1841, was of a promissory nature. The Rev. John Hopwood was appointed Treasurer, and Thomas Charles, Secretary to the Inspectors. In the Old Accrington Minute Book of 17th July, 1843, a resolution was agreed to that "the Inspectors of the township do, so far as they legally can, unite with the Inspectors appointed for lighting with gas the township of New Accrington, for the better carrying into effect the purposes of" the Act. The two later minute books together with one relating to Old Accrington, are in the Library, and the first entry concerning New Accrington relates to a meeting of the ratepayers, held in the National School on the 23rd October, 1846, with Mr. James Grimshaw in the chair. Six Inspectors were proposed, and the amount to be levied £170. Amendments to increase the number of Inspectors to eight and to reduce the amount to £70, were defeated. At a further meeting, on the 19th November, the six Inspectors were duly elected, and it is to be observed that Mr. Wm. Hutchinson, Book Printer and Stationer, and Mr. Enock Bowker, Bookseller and

Stationer, did all the moving and seconding of candidates. In 1848, the tender of the Directors of the Accrington Gas and Water Works Company, to supply gas at the rate of 48/- per lamp, was accepted. The Clerk to the Inspector (Mr. Charles) resigned in 1848, and Mr. Christopher West was appointed at the same salary (£8). The Gas Company later reduced their price per lamp to 47/-, possibly on account of the increase in the number of lights supplied, and again (in 1852), to 46/-. The Annual Accounts ranged from about £190 to £230, in these early years, and the amount of rate authorized to be levied from £150 to £190. The difference of £40 in each case was doubtless accounted for by the amount contributed from Old Accrington as their share of the cost. The rate levied for the year 1853, was £220, but this amount jumped to £500 the following year. It was at this period, August, 1853, that the consideration of the formation of a Fire Brigade took shape. Mr. Wm. Beesley was appointed Clerk to the Inspectors and Superintendent of the Fire Brigade. The minute book, commencing in 1846, previously referred to, contains copies of correspondence between Mr. Beesley and Mr. Rose, the Chief Superintendent of the Manchester Fire Establishment, the latter being called into consultation as to the fixing of the plugs and the supply of an engine and equipment. The Superintendent was authorized in September, 1853, to "proceed forthwith in securing 12 active men to be enrolled as a Fire Brigade." Rules governing the payment and management of Brigades were obtained from other authorities, and the Committee of the New Jerusalem Church were asked to allow the vaults to be used as an Engine House. Towards the cost of the Engine, House, and Brigade, New Accrington had to provide £340, and Old Accrington, £120. The New Jerusalem Committee evidently did not agree to the use of their premises for the purpose suggested, for in November, it was Resolved: "That the old warehouse, formerly occupied by Mr. James Cronshaw at the Old Mill in Grange Lane, be at once fitted up for an Engine House until another place can be obtained." Nor was this proposal a success, for in February, 1854, room was being sought at the "New Mill." The salary of the Superintendent received consideration this year, being fixed in April, at 8/- per week, and in July, the same year, at 12/- per week. The last entry recorded is an instruction, in February, 1855, to the

Inspector to "reduce the number of men so as to make the amount of money now on hand meet the expenses of the current year."

LOCAL BOARD OF HEALTH DAYS.

THE years 1850 to 1855, were exceedingly vital ones in the annals of the community. In them, the two divisions of Old and New Accrington were, to all intents and purposes, made one almost the only amalgamation scheme which has met with success. Petitions bearing the date 12th November, 1849, were sent by both townships to what was then the General Board of Health, with its offices at Gwydyr House, Whitehall, praying that a Superintending Inspector might be sent down to visit the townships and make public inquiry with a view to the adoption of the Public Health Act, 1848. The petition was signed by 56 ratepayers of Old, and 197 of New Accrington, and the Inspector appointed to conduct the inquiry was Benjamin Herschel Babbage. The inquiry was held in the Sessions Rooms during the 17th to the 23rd April, 1850. It was not allowed to be held without opposition, and, at the outset, question was raised as to its legality. The Inspector not only squashed this attempt but informed the opponents they were liable to a fine of £5 if they refused to appear before him or obstructed him in his duty. The leading gentlemen of the district including Messrs. Jonathan Peel, Robert Hargreaves, Jonathan Hargreaves, and the Rev. John Hopwood appeared in support of the application, and tribute is paid by the Inspector to the services rendered by Mr. Robert Redman, Relieving Officer, "who accompanied me during my local inspection, and bore with exemplary patience, the insults with which he was assailed by some badly-disposed persons, who took advantage of my inspection being a public one, to accompany me in my examination of the town." The Inspector noted that the number of obstructors was very small and their conduct in marked contrast to that of the other inhabitants, especially those of the poorer class. Mr. Wm. Beesley (who was clerk to the Lighting Inspectors) "upon the part of the opposers of the Public Health Act, accompanied me during my inspection of both places, for the purpose of watching my proceedings, and detecting any flaw which might occur in them," says the Inspector. The first section of the report gives a topographical and geological description of the area. In this connexion the plan of Accrington in 1849 is of great interest, as it

coincides with the date of the inquiry. The Inspector's description of the town may be compared with the plan. He says:
"Abbey Street, which is the principal street of the town, and runs parallel with the general direction of Hyndburn Brook, is situated upon the slope of the hill on the eastern side of the valley; from this street Warner Street, Oak Street, Blackburn Street, etc., branch off to the westward and run down to the brook. Bank Street, which runs in the same direction as Abbey Street, but between it and the brook intersects the above named streets. Blackburn Street is continued upon the western side of the Hyndburn Brook up the slope of the hill, and passes below the station of the East Lancashire Railway. Upon this side of the brook it takes the name of the Blackburn Road to which place it leads. A street, called Church Street, runs upon the western side of the brook from the lowest point of Blackburn Road towards the old Church of St. James's. There are many other small streets leading out of the main streets above mentioned, which it is not necessary to particularize, as a glance at the accompanying map will suffice to show their position. At the upper end of the town, the Warm den Brook is dammed up and forms several reservoirs which supply with water the Broad Oak Printworks. Upon the western side the Woodnook Water has been treated in a similar way, and supplies the reservoirs of the Messrs. Hargreaves' large cotton mill. The two streams join together near the bottom of Oak Street, and their united streams, after crossing Blackburn Street and receiving the waters of the Pleck Brook, flow in a north-westerly direction between Union Street and the Lower Fold, after which they finally leave the town, and take the direction of a village called Church." Having paid tribute to the general aspect of the town which, he says, "justifies the boast of its inhabitants that it is the cleanest town in Lancashire," he points out that the case is wholly reversed when dealing with the small unpaved back-yards, alleys, and courts containing pigsties and uncovered cesspits dotted about in every direction "open drains are found running in immediate vicinity to the houses." Although a great many new houses had been built, or were in course of building, their planning and sanitary arrangement did not meet with the Inspector's approval, and justified "the observation of one of the promoters of the inquiry that the application of the Public Health Act was required as much for the prevention of future evils in new buildings. . . . as for the remedying of existing ones." Much of the

land around Accrington he describes as very wet, and points out that "in the cellars of several of the houses in the Higher Fold, which is near the brook, there are wells of soft water which the inhabitants use for domestic purposes, but few of them in this locality being supplied by the water company."

No nearer rain-gauge than that at Stonyhurst College, was then in existence, and the average for the four years, 1846-1849, is given as 43.895 inches.

The report goes on to say that "Accrington has no corporation or other governing body, having only lately risen into importance, which has been caused chiefly by the great increase of the population, brought together by the establishment of large printworks and cotton mills in the neighbourhood." It also outlines the provision of the Act authorizing the promotion of the Gas and Water Company.

It is stated that the approximate number of persons engaged at factories, about one quarter of the population, is as follows:

Messrs. Hargreaves & Co., Broad Oak Print Works	850
Messrs. J. Grimshaw & Co., Plantation Mill Print Works	169
Mr. Cronkshaw's Cotton Factory	43
Messrs. Cunliffe & Co.	100
Messrs. Hargreaves'	755
Mr. Thompson's	85
Mr. Whitehead's	70
Mr. Priestley's Cotton Factory	40
Mr. Walmesley's Cotton Factory	250
Messrs. Massey & Clegg's	100
Total	2,462

The population of the two townships was estimated at 10,813 (the census return for 1851, gives 10,376. Conclusions are drawn from the mortality returns in favour of the petitioners the death rate is given as: New Accrington, 22.1 per 1,000; Old Accrington, 22.7 per 1,000; the average of all England at that time being 21.85 to-day (1927) it is 14.6.

— CENTRE OF

ACCRINGTON
OLD ACCRINGTON
WHALLEY ROAD
ABBEY STREET
BANK STREET
HINDBURN
CHURCH ST
ST JAMES STREET
NORTH
SCALE OF YARDS

ACCRINGTON 1849.
EAST
WEST.
SOUTH.
HARGREAVES STREET
SPRING GARDENS
ABBEY STREET
BANK STREET
WARNER STREET
CROSS STREET
CHURCH STREET
WELLINGTON STREET
ACCRINGTON.
OLD ACCRINGTON
SCAITCLIFFE LANE
EAST LANCASHIRE RAILWAY

The figures for Out-door relief for the two years 1849 and 1850, are given as £2,098 8s. 10d., "one-fifth of which was occasioned by the sickness and premature mortality of able-bodied labourers."

The Annual Value of Property in New Accrington, was £20,886 11s. 0d., in Old Accrington, £6,341 16s. 0d., a total of £27,228 7s. 0d.: the Rateable values respectively being £18,201 0s. 8d., and £5,516 7s. 8d.

There were 1,562 houses under £10 value, 91 above that value, 14 inns and public houses, 96 shops and beerhouses, eight cotton mills, three bleachworks, and four printworks. The return of public houses and beershops is amplified later and given as 41, "one house in every 47 devoted to the sale of beer and spirits." The Rates levied during 1849, were £1,935 11s. 11d.

THE OLD PUMP, PENNYHOUSE.

It was not very creditable to the town that there were 678 cesspits and refuse heaps, 124 houses with only one room, 66 pigsties containing pigs, and 126 empty pigsties that the latter were empty was due to the zeal of Mr. Redman, the Inspector of Nuisances, and a tribute to the Nuisances Removal Act. There seems to have been justification for Mr. Babbage's view that a stronger local governing body, insisting upon better housing and drainage, would not only assist in saving life, but add to the efficiency of the labourers. Mr. Redman had no easy task, one-third of his notices were ignored and many of the defects were only temporarily remedied, and in a very superficial manner. The report criticises the drainage system very severely: it is dealt with later under Sewerage. His description of some of the cesspits will hardly bear thinking about to-day: evidence of slum property sufficient to satisfy any Parliamentary Committee could have been supplied. The report of the condition of Old Accrington compares favourably with that of New Accrington, but reference is made to the presence of two ponds which lay between the garden of Mr. Hall's house in St. James's Street and the railway; ponds which presented a surface of some 1,300 yards of green stagnant water, concerning which Mr. Hall justly complained. The whole of the drainage emptied itself into the river Hyndburn, or, Accrington Brook.

There follows a description of the domestic arrangements of several houses. Of one sleeping-room in Daisy Hill, it is said: "Four of the fourteen persons sleeping in this room consist of children stated to be taken in for a few days only." They had gone apparently, for a change of air. 194 persons were sleeping nightly in places where the average cubic feet of space allowed to each person was only 213. Again Old Accrington was ahead, the average being 247 cubic feet.

778 houses were not supplied with water directly laid on. Some had wells in their cellars, others paid a small rent for leave to draw water from a private well, but by far the largest number fetched their water from public wells or springs, of which there were several in different parts of the town. One of the best remembered being the Gambo Well, near the bottom of Burnley Road.

The Inspector's report was whole-heartedly in favour of permission being granted to adopt the Public Health Act. His report contains a recommendation on the subject of amalgamation which might have been read into recent proceedings on this subject. "As the two townships of New and Old Accrington are so intimately connected together, as the boundaries between them are so interlaced, and as they form substantially part of the same drainage area, there can be no doubt but that they should form part of the same district, and thus the expenses of two separate Boards, with separate offices, would be dispensed with. I recommend, therefore, that the two townships of New and Old Accrington be incorporated together, for the purposes of the Public Health Act, into the new district of Accrington."

The Inspector was a man of vision. After outlining his ideas of a sewage scheme he concludes: "Thus the Sanitary Reformer, energetically sweeping away all that is detrimental to the physical health, will pave the way for the entrance of that ray of light which will usher the Teacher and the Minister into those dark corners of our crowded towns, from which the atmosphere of miasma and the positive state of filth, has hitherto effectually barred them out."

We have given this somewhat lengthy account of the condition of Accrington in the middle of the nineteenth century, first, because it gives plain unbiased views of its conditions by one fully qualified to judge, and, secondly, because in this Jubilee Year it is, perhaps, well to remind ourselves of the conditions of our townspeople when the first real attempt towards town's government was being urged. Thirdly, in that as this volume contains a full account of the municipal activities of the town a true comparison, then and now, may be made.

A second inquiry was held at Accrington, September 22nd, 1852, to determine the future boundary of the district for the purposes of the Public Health Act.

The Act to confirm the Provisional Order of the General Board of Health for Accrington, dated 20th August, 1853 (16 and 17 Victoria, 126), was passed. This authorized the first election to take place on the 31st August the same year, the Board to consist of eighteen persons. Robert Hargreaves, of Bank House, was authorized to perform the duties vested in, or imposed upon, the Chairman of the Local Board of Health, or, failing him, James Grimshaw, Plantation Mills. Many of the actual documents concerning the election, signed by Mr. Robert Hargreaves, are in the care of the Public Library, and it is hoped to arrange an exhibition of these during the Jubilee Celebrations.

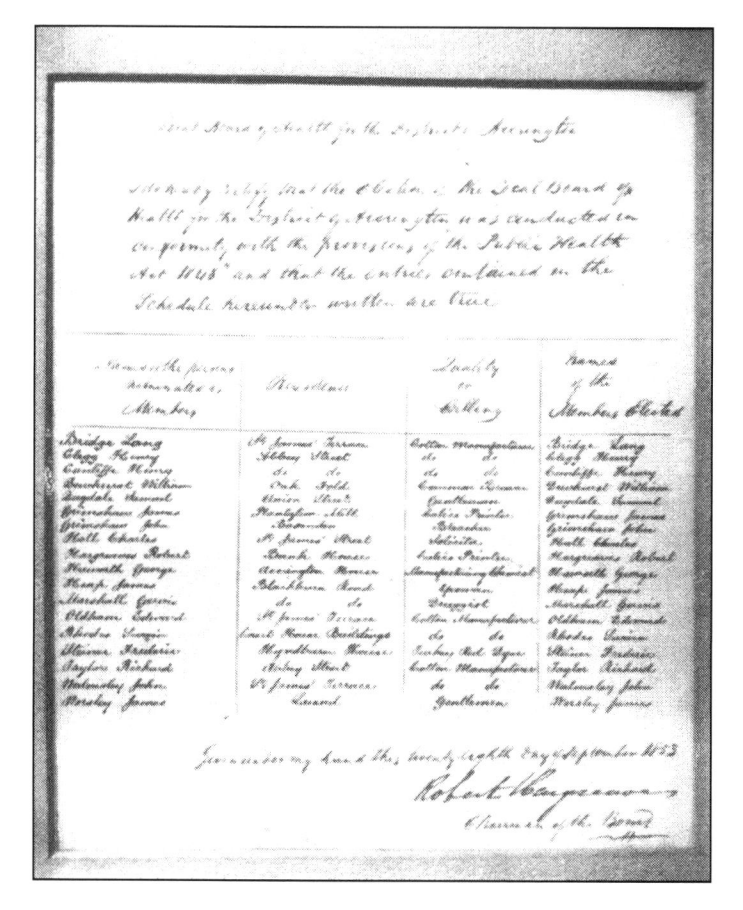

CERTIFICATE OF ELECTION OF THE FIRST LOCAL BOARD OF HEALTH.

As an example, there is here reproduced the actual certificate of the election of the first Board attested by the Chairman:

Mr. George Bannister was appointed Clerk to the Board.

The record of the Board's achievements is no mean one. Consider the state of the town at the time of Mr. Babbage's report, and it must be admitted the Board handed over the reins of power to the 1878 Council with no reason to be ashamed of the improvements effected.

The early efforts of the Board were chiefly devoted to cleansing the town of the imperfections referred to by Mr. Babbage, and to enforcing adherence to the bye-laws they early adopted: particularly breaches of the building bye-laws. It was not until 1854, that the Clerk's salary was agreed upon he was passing rich on £40 a year, but was paid extra for professional (legal) services. An instruction was given to apply to Captain Woodford for terms upon which the Sessions Room at the Police Court might be used for the Board's meetings, the agreed rent being £5 per annum.

The officials in addition to the Clerk were Collector (£20) with a fidelity bond of £500, Surveyor (£50), and Inspector of Nuisances (£10). Arrangements were made with a farmer to remove the refuse for £30. The early Committees appointed were Lighting, Finance, Building and Nuisances, and General Purposes followed, these were only slightly altered later, and added to as occasion arose. Mr. Robert Hargreaves did not attend many meetings his death occurring in May, 1854. The Gas and Water Co.'s undertaking caused considerable discussion, and the Board did not oppose the Co.'s Parliamentary bill, which included clauses allowing the Local Board the power to purchase. Mr. James Grimshaw succeeded Mr. Hargreaves and occupied the chair for six years.

Compounding for the payment of rates was agreed to (for property under £10 in value) in 1855, and it was towards the end of this year that a movement was made for a Sewerage Scheme. In the following year (1856), sanction to borrow £4,800 for this scheme, was granted.

THE OLD COURT HOUSE.

From the number of times it was resolved to "adjourn to the Clerk's office," one is led to the conclusion that this was equivalent to dismissing the press, and meeting in private; indeed, the Board resolved later to consider at each meeting whether they would conduct the business in privacy or not. Wm. Grime was appointed Collector and Inspector at £45, and to these offices he added that of Surveyor the next year, at an inclusive salary of £75. The General District Rate estimate in 1857 was: Salaries, £115; Highways, £300; Lighting, £270; Miscellaneous, £30; Total, £715. The precursor of the Town's Yard was in Blackburn Road, near the southerly end of Union Street the portion used being "fenced off." The Clerk was succeeded in 1857 by Henry Edge (of Blackburn), afterwards by R. Massey; G. Bannister being re-appointed in 1860, at £80. There were minor offences against the peace in those days, for notices had to be posted "cautioning persons against playing at Buck Stick, Tip Ball, and other games, and pigeon keepers against throwing stones also against the obstruction of foot-paths by perambulators."

MR. JAS. GRIMSHAW, CHAIRMAN, L.B.H., 1854-60.

1858 saw a move towards the establishment of a cemetery. Dr. Holland, Government Inspector of Burial Grounds, made an inspection of Christ Church ground at the request of the Vicar (Rev. Featherstone), with a view to extensions. The Inspector asked the Board's view, which was against the proposal even when it was suggested to use the extension only for vaults and walled graves. The Local Board sought and obtained powers to become a Burial Board, held a town's meeting, and eventually made a general order for the closing of Burial Grounds, though this could not have been fully effective or intended to be immediately, as the Cemetery was not opened until 1864, and St. James's Churchyard remained open until December, 1866. Trouble was experienced in 1858, with the Lighting and Watching Inspectors, but they eventually gave up the Fire Engine, Hose, Books, and Cash, but did not readily part with the latter. The firemen were engaged by the Board, henceforth Fire Brigade business was considerable.

1859 was an important year in Accrington's local history. A meeting of the inhabitants of Old and New Accrington was held at the Peel Institution on Saturday, March 12th, with Mr. Benjamin Hargreaves in the Chair, when the following resolution was unanimously adopted: "That in the opinion of this meeting, it is desirable that the townships of Old and New Accrington, and suitable portions of the adjoining townships, should be constituted a parliamentary Borough, and that this meeting pledges itself to make every effort to accomplish that object. "Mr. Geo. Bannister was appointed Secretary, and he lost no time in calling the Committee together. A petition was presented to Parliament in favour of Accrington, Church, Clayton, Huncoat, and Oswaldtwistle, being constituted a Parliamentary Borough. The proposal was not successful, and a second one was presented in 1867, but it was not until the 1885 election that the old North-East Lancashire Division was divided and Accrington District sent its member to Parliament.

In this year also (1859), a Petition was presented to the Poor Law Commissioners in favour of the formation of a new Union made up of portions of the Blackburn, Burnley, and Haslingden Unions to include Greater Accrington, Harwood, and Rishton, and covering a population of 27,889, of which number Accrington totalled 10,376. Commenting upon this matter, the "Blackburn Weekly Times" gave its blessing to the proposal, but expressed doubt of its success. It was, as everyone knows, not successful.

The bye-laws were revised in 1859, after lengthy discussion a copy may be seen in the Library. In this year the cost of removal of refuse had risen to £85. It seems curious in these days of secret voting, to find the Board deciding which of their number should retire at the end of the year: it would be an excellent opportunity for ridding themselves of an obnoxious member. The Board also filled vacancies, and there is a curious fact in nomenclature recorded, the two nominees for a vacancy being Ingham and Bingham-B. won. Street lighting at this period cost 40/- per lamp.

In 1861, Mr. Swain Rhodes was elected Chairman, and served for two terms of three years each, 1861-63 and 1871-73.

MR. SWAIN RHODES,
CHAIRMAN L.B.H.,
1861-3 AND 1871.

MR. WILLIAM
DEWHURST, CHAIRMAN
L.B.H., 1864.

In October, 1861, the Board was definitely made a Burial Board. The widening of "Black Bull Bridge" was a topic for discussion, continuing until 1865, when the County Magistrates' Committee made a grant of £250 towards the cost.

The period of the reign of the Board covered the terrible days of distress caused by the Cotton Famine, commencing in the autumn of 1861, and lasting some three years. A Relief Committee was appointed in March, 1862.

Extensive borrowing powers were sought "for permanent works proposed to be carried out," £30,000 being asked for. The town had extensive alterations in view: the purchase of the Peel Institution, the erection of a Market House (authority being secured at a town's meeting on November 28th, 1863), and Slaughter Houses.

MR. JAS. BARLOW, CHAIRMAN L.B.H., 1865.

The General District Rate Estimate had increased to £2,472 in 1864 1s. 6d. in the £ on buildings, and 4½d. on land. The Chairman at that period was Mr. William Dewhurst. In this year it was resolved: "That the Collector summon the first ratepayer who refuses to pay the Board's rate on account of alleged illegality."

In 1865 (under the Chairmanship of Mr. James Barlow), the Local Board purchased the Peel Institution, now the Town Hall, for the sum of £4,000: no doubt there would be Jeremiahs in those days who would complain of this squandering of public monies. Time has proved how important and valuable this purchase was. Agreement was constantly sought and sometimes reached with the Turnpike Trust as to the repair of roads.

Much of the Board's time was taken up in 1865-66, with arrangements for the purchase of property for the Market Site, one design being approved in July, 1866, and with the important topic of arching the Hyndburn River (or Brook).

SITE OF THE MARKET HALL.

Another important project of the Local Board was the erection of the Market Hall. This must have been a big undertaking in those days for Accrington, but its worth has been proved and it is a monument to the foresight of the town's rulers. In 1867, Mr. John F. Doyle's plans were definitely accepted, and he was appointed to "superintend until the completion of the whole works in connection with the erection of the New Market House, at the rate of five per cent. on an estimated expenditure of £6,500, this percentage to be accepted in full for the superintendence, travelling expenses, and the preparation of all the necessary specifications in connection with the said works." It was not erected without controversy: the Library contains a plan of the "proposed Market Hall," indicating the lines of certain land which was to be given as compensation for other land

and bearing the admonition "Judge for yourselves." The Market Hall was opened by Mr. Samuel Dugdale, Chairman of the Board, on October 23rd, 1869. Richard Moore was appointed Market Inspector, at 6/- per week.

THE MARKET HALL.

Mr. R. H. Rowland was appointed Treasurer in March, 1868, and held the position until January, 1904, but history does not say who was appointed by the Surveyor in carrying out an instruction "to engage a boy that can write."

Towards the end of this year (1868) the association of the magistrates and police with the occupancy of the Town Hall commenced portions being rented to them.

It is of interest to note that two gentlemen closely connected with the religious life of the community came to Accrington in the same year (1869), the Rev. Canon Rogers (Vicar of Accrington, 1869-1905), and the Rev. Charles Williams (Baptist Minister, 1869-1901). Both had a long and honourable association with the town.

Both were champions of the rights of their respective denominations, as the published pamphlets of the day prove.

MR. SAMUEL DUGDALE, CHAIRMAN, L.B.H., 1866-69.

REV. JOHN ROGERS.  THE REV. CHARLES WILLIAMS.

MR. GEORGE W. BARLOW, CHAIRMAN, L.B.H., 1870.

In 1869, new offices for the Board and their Staffs were considered: these were built and let to the magistrates at the close of 1870 when Mr. Geo. W. Barlow was chairman. The magistrates entered upon their tenancy on January 1st, 1871, paying £125 rent (inclusive of the rooms at the Peel Institution).

It must have been quite an epoch in the history of the town when the local toll-bars were abolished in October, 1871. A motorist (in Wales or Scotland chiefly), when called upon to pay for the right of taking his car over some of the toll-bridges to-day, realizes to some extent what must have been the feelings of travellers in the olden days on arriving at toll-bars. The Trusts ceased entirely in 1875. A further step in the direction of reform was made in 1872 when, following upon the report of a Special Committee of the Board upon the sanitary condition of some parts of the town, from which it would appear that the reforms suggested in 1850 had not been effected too hurriedly, the decision was reached that all cellar dwellings be closed. This order was to take effect as from the first of May, 1872.

In 1873, the question of creating Accrington a new Petty Sessional Division was considered at the Preston Quarter Sessions on the 1st January, following upon a requisition. The request was agreed to by a majority of 21 votes to four.

The Board, in 1874, took into serious consideration the conditions under which animals were slaughtered, and the need for supplying public baths. It was decided, after much discussion, to purchase Pleck Meadow Estate for this dual reform. The project, however, did not mature, though the site was considered eminently suited to the first-named object on account of its proximity to the railway station.

About this period, signs were evident that the town was looking to some extension of the scope of its authority. It was growing rapidly in size and the live members of the Board realized that Incorporation would give them authority and status, which they did not possess as a Local Board.

MR. WILLIAM GREEN, CHAIRMAN L.B.H., 1876.

INCORPORATION.

THE question of Incorporation was considered at a Town's Meeting, held in the Peel Institution on Monday, July 31st. Mr. Wm. Green, Chairman of the Local Board in 1876, presided. The proposal: "That in the opinion of this meeting of the inhabitant householders of Old and New Accrington, it is expedient to promote the incorporation of the town of Accrington," was moved by Mr. Thomas Hindle and seconded by Mr. Robert Hargreaves. The report makes interesting reading, some of the arguments sound quite familiar increase in rates, salary of the Mayor to be used in entertaining the Council, reckless expenditure on borough police, increase in the Town Clerk's salary. The proposal was carried with only four dissentients.

The town's petition was heard, and Accrington was constituted a Municipal Borough.

The charter setting forth this privilege is dated 15th February, 1878, and reads as follows: VICTORIA BY THE GRACE OF GOD of the United Kingdom of Great Britain and Ireland Queen Defender of the Faith TO ALL TO WHOM these presents shall come, Greeting, WHEREAS by the Municipal Corporations (now Charters) Act, 1877, it was enacted that, if on the petition to Her Majesty of the inhabitant householders of any town or towns or districts in England or of any of these inhabitants praying for a grant of a Charter of Incorporation, Her Majesty by the advice of Her Privy Council thinks fit by charter to create such town towns or districts or any part thereof specified in the charter with or without any adjoining place a municipal borough and to incorporate the inhabitants thereof, it should be lawful for Her Majesty by the charter to extend to that municipal borough and the inhabitants thereof so incorporated the provisions of the Municipal Corporations Acts and that every petition for a charter under that Act should be referred to a Committee of the Lords of Her Majesty's Privy Council (in the Act referred to as the Committee "of Council") AND WHEREAS certain inhabitant householders of the town and townships of Old and New Accrington in the County of Lancaster have petitioned Us for the grant of a Charter of Incorporation AND WHEREAS such petition was referred to a Committee of Our Privy Council and one month at least before the same was taken into consideration by the said Committee notice thereof and of the time when the same was so to be taken into consideration was duly published in the "London Gazette" as directed by the Committee AND WHEREAS Our Privy Council have recommended Us to grant this Charter of Incorporation WE THEREFORE as well by virtue of Our Royal Prerogative as of the power given to us by the Municipal Corporations (now Charters) Act, 1877, or any other act and of all other power and authorities enabling Us in this behalf by the advise of Our Privy Council DO hereby grant and declare as follows:

1. The inhabitants of the town and townships of Old and New Accrington within the limits set forth in the first schedule to these presents and their successors shall be one body politic and corporate by the name of the Mayor Aldermen and Burgesses of the Borough of Accrington with perpetual succession and a Common Seal and may assume Armorial Bearings (which shall be duly enrolled in the Heralds College) and may take and hold such lands and hereditaments within the Borough as may be necessary for the site of the buildings and premises required for the official purposes of the Corporation and other the purposes of the said Municipal Corporation Acts.

2. The Mayor Aldermen and Burgesses of the said Borough shall have the powers authorities immunities and privileges usually invested by law in the Mayor Aldermen and Burgesses of a Municipal Borough and the provisions of the said Municipal Corporations Acts shall extend to the said Borough and the inhabitants thereof incorporated by this Charter.

The remaining sections of the Charter deal with the number of councillors and their election, etc.

The Charter included the right to bear arms, and the Coat-of-Arms granted by the Heralds' College appears as the frontispiece to this volume, and their authority to use it is here reproduced.

THE CHARTER OF INCORPORATION.

Accrington proceeded to elect its first Councillors, and it must have been an election worth witnessing. Much of the election literature of the time is preserved at the Library, every second line appears to contain matter for a libel action. In one, the electors are warned and advised: "If you want members who don't fall asleep while business is proceeding, don't vote for "The result of the election on April 24th, 1878 was a complete victory for the Liberal Party, and defeat of the "Non-political candidates."

The first meeting of the Town Council was held on the 9th May, Alderman Lightfoot being elected the first Mayor. Its progress municipally, herein set forth departmentally, is such that none may feel anything but "great pride in what has been attained," and amply bears out the remarks of the Jubilee Mayor, Alderman T. E. Higham, at the Jubilee Meeting of the present Council, on the 9th May, 1928.

During its fifty years of Incorporation the Borough has not elected anyone to Freemanship, but it is commencing its second fifty years by marking the services of the Jubilee Mayor and his long association with the social and municipal life of the community, by conferring upon him the distinction of being the first Freeman of the Borough.

ALDERMAN JOHN E. LIGHTFOOT, FIRST MAYOR OF ACCRINGTON.

Photo by Tattersall.

TOWN COUNCIL IN 1880.

The names reading from left to right are :

Standing : Wm. Maden, Thos. Hindle, John Wilkinson, James Barlow, Thomas Holgate, Jos. Broughton, Wm. Ramsbottom, Dr. Clayton, William Smith, James Barlow, Wm. Clegg, Henry Cunliffe, Eli Higham, John Riley, Rev. Joseph Dawson (Chaplain), Dr. Milne (Medical Officer), Edmund Riley.

Seated : James Whittaker, Bridge Baron, R. H. Rowland (Treasurer), W. Entwisle, Thomas Howarth, Edmund Whittaker (Town Clerk), J. E. Lightfoot (Mayor), Swain Rhodes, F. N. Haywood, Lowther Ward, Gervase Marshall.

Seated on ground : Eli Knowles (Surveyor), James Kenyon, Williamson Lee, Thomas Whittaker, Enoch Crabtree

ALDERMAN T.E. HIGHAM, JUBILEE MAYOR.

MRS. T.E. HIGHAM, JUBILEE MAYORESS.

GROUP OF MAYORS, 1878 TO 1928.

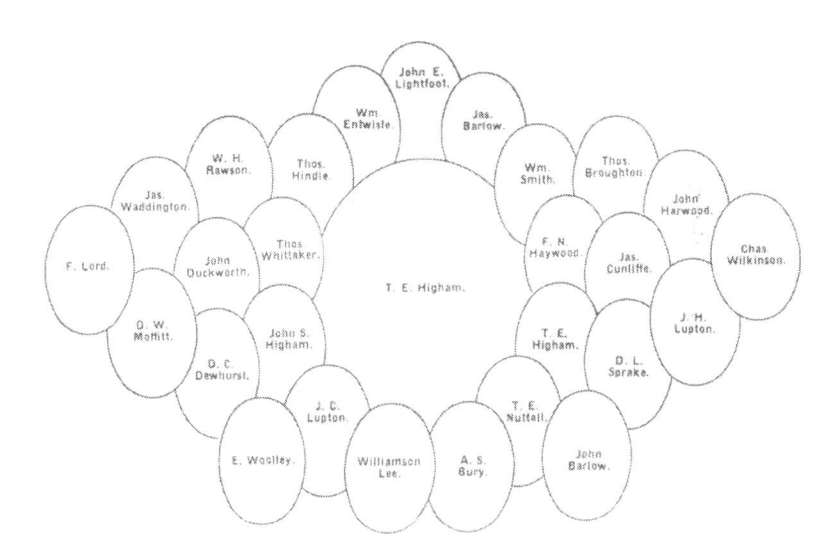

John E. Lightfoot.
Wm Entwisle.
Jas. Barlow.
W. H. Rawson.
Thos. Hindle.
Wm. Smith.
Thos. Broughton.
Jas. Waddington.
John Harwood.
F. Lord.
John Duckworth.
Thos. Whittaker.
F. N. Haywood.
Jas. Cunliffe.
Chas. Wilkinson.
T. E. Higham.
O. W. Moffitt.
John S. Higham.
T. E. Higham.
J. H. Lupton.
D. C. Dewhurst.
D. L. Sprake.
J. C. Lupton.
T. E. Nuttall.
E. Woolley.
Williamson Lee.
A. S. Bury.
John Barlow.

91

THE TOWN COUNCIL, 1928.

Photo by Tattersall.

The names reading from left to right are:

Front Row: Coun. W. A. Lambert, Coun. R. Watson, Ald. J. Sudall, Ald. A. S. Bury, Ald. W. H. Rawson, Ald. T. E. Higham (Mayor), Mr. W. H. Warhurst (Town Clerk), Ald. C. Wilkinson, Ald. J. Barlow, Ald. J. Waddington, Ald. G. H. Ellis, Coun. J. S. Snell.

Middle Row: Coun. J. Lord, Coun. O. Wade, Coun. R. I. Constantine, Coun. J. Barlow, Mr. H. Knowles (Mayor's Attendant), Coun. J. W. Tasker, Coun. W. Whittaker, Coun. A. E. Higham, Coun. W. H. Roberts, Coun. J. Laytham.

Coun. G. D. M. Beaton, Coun. A. Wilkinson, Coun. J. H. Priestley, Coun. G. E. Slack, Coun. B. Robinson, Coun. C. Livesey, Coun. S. Sutcliffe,

Back Row: Coun. J. Whittaker, Coun. J. Baron, Coun. T. O'Connor, Coun. W. E. Woolley, Coun. J. S. Harbinson.

92

THE CORPORATION OFFICIALS, 1928, WITH DATE OF APPOINTMENT TO PRESENT POSITION.

Photo by Tattersall.

The names reading from left to right are:

Front Row: J. Spencer, School Attendance Officer (1897); A. T. Townsend, Cemetery Registrar (1910); H. Boyd, Parks Superintendent (1914); R. Porter, Horse Keeper (1896); G. Sinclair, Chief Constable (1903); A. Greenhalgh, Medical Officer of Health (1899); W. H. Wachurst, Town Clerk (1926); E. L. Lever, Borough Treasurer (1920); W. Howell, Director of Education (1927); J. W. Clayton, Valuation Officer and Chief Collector (1923); C. W. Eskins, Head Master of the Grammar School (1920); W. Mawdsley, Gasworks Manager (1925).

Back Row: J. W. Singleton, Borough Librarian (1901); A. Hanson, Museum Curator (1922); A. W. Clegg, Electrical Engineer (1917); A. A. Crabtree, School Attendance Officer (1928); T. H. Rawcliffe, Baths Superintendent (1913); J. A. Kindle, Sanitary Inspector (1927); H. Sanderson, Borough Surveyor (1928); H. Piling, Tramways Manager (1911); H. Knowles, Town Hall Keeper (1916); F. Lomax, School Dentist (1928); W. J. Heard, Deputy Borough Surveyor (1914); J. T. Aspden, Markets Inspector (1912).

MR. A.H. AITKEN, TOWN CLERK 1885-1926.

MR. W.H. WARHURST, PRESENT TOWN CLERK.

TOWN CLERK'S DEPARTMENT.

ONE of the first duties of the new Borough was the appointment of Town Clerk, and Mr. Edmund Whittaker, who had previously held the position of Clerk to the old Local Board (formed in 1853), was appointed at the first meeting.

After remaining in the office for a period of seven years, he was succeeded by Mr. Arthur Henry Aitken, on the 1st June, 1885, and that gentleman served the town for upwards of 41 years, retiring on the 31st August, 1926, he being in turn succeeded by Mr William Henry Warhurst, LL.B., the present Town Clerk.

During the period referred to, many changes and developments have taken place and the progress made may to some extent, be gauged by making a comparison of the Standing Committees which existed at the Incorporation with those now constituted.

The Committees formed at the first meeting of the Council after Incorporation were the General Works, Health, Watch and Cemetery, Town Hall and Market, School Attendance, and Finance.

Whilst these Committees have continued to function up to the present day, with, in certain instances, slightly altered titles, many others have been added from time to time, namely, Electricity and Tramways, Baths and Libraries, Parks, Stables, Education, Old Age Pensions, Maternity and Child Welfare, Housing, Parliamentary, and Rating and Valuation.

In addition, the Council is largely represented on two Joint Boards, namely, the Accrington District Gas and Water Board and the Accrington and Church Joint Outfall Sewerage Board.

The only Municipal Buildings or Undertakings of importance owned by the Corporation in the year 1878, were the Town Hall, Market, and the Cemetery, the latter having been opened so far back as 1864.

The details of the municipal progress which has taken place, are surveyed in this souvenir. They form a record of which the inhabitants may well feel proud, especially having regard to the fact that Accrington is by no means so heavily rated as most industrial towns.

The addition of all these undertakings has, of course, added enormously to the duties and responsibilities of the Town Clerk's Department, and whilst each Department has its separate head, this Department is responsible for all the legal and a certain proportion of the administrative work in connexion therewith.

The Town Clerk is appointed pursuant to Act of Parliament, and is the Chief Executive Officer. He is the legal adviser, performs all duties appertaining to the office of Clerk to the Town Council, acting as the Urban, Sanitary, Burial, Education, and Housing Authority for the Borough, is Registration Officer and Acting Returning Officer for the Parliamentary Borough of Accrington, and has charge of the Local Land Charges Register. The Town Clerk also acts as Clerk to the Rating Authority under the Rating and

Valuation Act, 1925. He acts as Solicitor in the promotion of or opposition to Local Bills and Provisional Orders. In addition, the Town Clerk is usually entrusted with the negotiations for the acquisition of lands and properties for various Corporate purposes.

In the legal branch, the Town Clerk is the official to make all searches, peruse and investigate all titles, compare all deeds, prepare conveyances, mortgages, transfers, contracts, notices, and other documents; see to the making and levying of rates, the proper sealing and execution of all deeds and documents, have the custody of all the legal documents of the Corporation, and all other books, papers, and documents relating to his office.

One of the most important duties of the Town Clerk is to advise the several officers and servants of the Corporation in all matters pertaining to their respective duties in relation to the affairs of the Corporation, exercise a general supervision over all the departments of the Corporation, and report to the Councilor to the appropriate Committee thereof on all matters which he considers should be brought before them, whether such matters arise in his own or any other department.

Another sphere of duty in the Town Clerk's position is in relation to Criminal Law and Practice where he advises the Chief Constable on all matters relating to prosecutions, informations, and complaints, which may be initiated by the Police, and conducts such cases if desirable in the Police Court or any subsequent Court.

The Town Clerk is also expected to convene and attend (as far as practicable) all Council, Committee, and Sub-Committee meetings, and is responsible for the minutes of such meetings and the correspondence arising thereupon.

When required, he must advise the Mayor in all matters appertaining to his official duties, and accompany him on occasions when the Mayor is in attendance at any function in his official capacity. Much of the correspondence and secretarial work of the Mayor in connection with his social and charitable activities is dealt with in the Town Clerk's office, as well as the legal and administrative work involved in the carrying on of movements inaugurated by previous Mayors.

HIGHWAYS.

THE main roads through the town, with the exception of Abbey Street, which was sett paved, were formed with ordinary water bound macadam for some years after the incorporation of the Borough. Blackburn Road and Whalley Road were afterwards principally paved with granite setts on concrete foundations, the chief exception being a length of wood paving opposite the Town Hall and Market Hall which, after about 25 years' wear was replaced last year with a modern "Lithocrete" surface. Burnley Road and Manchester Road continued as macadam roads in various forms until paved with granite setts on concrete foundation, the work being completed in each case last year.

In 1850, according to the report of Mr. Babbage, the "new" streets were in a bad condition, chiefly on account of the property owners making them in a variety of ways, and that the law as then existing, was insufficient to secure a better state of affairs.

It is interesting to note that each township had a road surveyor, and that the cost of highway repairs for three years was as follows:

YEAR.	TOWNSHIP OF NEW ACCRINGTON.			TOWNSHIP OF OLD ACCRINGTON.		
	£	s.	d.	£	s.	d.
Year ending in the spring of 1848	285	10	8	109	17	5
Do. 1849	176	17	11	77	17	1
Do. 1850	116	9	9	69	2	3

Note the decreasing cost of maintenance each year.

The making up of new streets in the rapidly growing town would probably continue in the haphazard fashion described until the passing of the Public Health Act of 1875, which gave power to enforce better construction before the Corporation took over the maintenance. These pre 1875 "new" streets have always been a source of trouble on account of the insufficient foundation, and in many cases a complete absence of any at all. With the coming of Mr. Newton, as Borough Engineer, in 1888, a sound policy for the making up of private streets was evolved and rigidly adhered to.

MR. W.J. NEWTON, BOROUGH SURVEYOR, 1888-1928.

The carriageways of the front streets are paved with grit setts on rubble pitching or concrete foundation, with kerbed and flagged footpaths on each side, while the back streets are similarly paved with a centre channel with an 18 inch wide kerb footway on each side.

Now, Accrington will compare most favourably with any town for its wellpaved streets and the reasonable annual maintenance costs of its highways.

There are 55.31 miles of highways within the Borough maintained by the Corporation, which may be summarized as follows:

MAIN ROADS, classified by the Ministry of Transport as First Class:
Blackburn Road, Peel Street, and Burnley Road
A.679
Blackburn Road (commercial Hotel to Abbey Street)
A.6065
Manchester Road, Abbey Street, and Whalley Road
A.680

4.81 miles.

MAIN ROADS, classified by the Ministry of Transport as Second Class:
King Street and Castle Stree B.6236
Queen's Road B.6237

70 miles.

DISTRICT ROADS (which includes 3.10 miles of Secondary Roads as follows:
Willows Lane, Hyndburn Road, Dale Street, Lower Antley Street, Lonsdale Street, Pickup Street, and Spring Hill Road)

49.80 miles.

55.31 miles

GRANGE LANE.

PUBLIC STREET IMPROVEMENTS AND DEVELOPMENT.

THE formation of the turnpike roads through Accrington about the end of the eighteenth century, was the first development towards a better system of highways. This is obvious when one considers the splendid lines upon which these roads were constructed, with greatly improved gradients to those in existence on the older roads through the two townships, such as Hollins Lane, Grange Lane (before its improvement), Weir Street, Kenyon Street, Milnshaw Lane, etc.

Grange Lane is one of the oldest thoroughfares in the town, and, with its continuation Hollins Lane the old road to Manchester from Clitheroe. These roads Manchester Road, Whalley Road, Blackburn Road, and Burnley Road are the main lines upon which the development of the town has taken place. Peel Street, laid out on the old private carriage road of the Peels, from Accrington House gateway to St. James's Church, is the most important connecting link in the centre of the town between the original turnpike roads, and is now classed along with them as "First Class" under the present Ministry of Transport's grading scheme of roads.

Towards the end of the nineteenth century, and later, it has been found necessary to widen these main roads in many parts, the most important being that of Blackburn Road from Peel Street to Eagle Street. New property has been erected along; this road, which to-day, forms a modern shopping thoroughfare which will bear comparison with any town, and the completion of which is a splendid tribute to the foresight and enterprise of the Councils of this period, and their officials. Peel Street has also been widened to a general width of 16 yards. That this progressive policy will be continued is assured by the fact that the present Council is seeking to secure the necessary powers in the Bill now before Parliament to complete the widening of the main roads.

Other notable improvements which have been made are (1) Grange Lane and Syke Street, which involved the demolition of much old property, the culverting of the stream, and the raising of the level of the roadway. Amongst the property demolished was the Old Black Dog Inn, which was situated at the bottom of Nuttall Street, formerly known as Woodnook Lane. (2) The continuation of Oak Street to Cannon Street, forming a most useful bye-pass road to the Station. (3) King Street, near Bull Bridge, which is now classified by the Ministry of Transport as "Second Class" by reason of its being a valuable connecting route between Blackburn Road and Whalley Road.

HIGHER GRANGE LANE.

Many other effective widenings and improvements have been carried out on other thoroughfares in the town.

The greatest public improvement which remains to be done, is the continuation of Marquis Street, from Whalley Road through the site of Spring Mill into Union Street at the Police Station. The construction of this work will provide an alternative artery for traffic through the centre of the town. It will create valuable frontages for the Town Hall extension scheme, for shops, and other business properties, and afford possible facilities for an adequate motor bus centre.

CORNER OF BLACKBURN ROAD: SITE OF BRIDGE'S SHOP.

PICCADILLY BEFORE ALTERATIONS.

CORNER OF BLACKBURN ROAD AND ABBEY STREET.

THE OLD BLACK DOG INN.

QUEEN'S ROAD BEFORE DEVELOPMENT.

Estate development has also proceeded on sound lines in spite of the many difficulties encountered, such as topographical features, the position of the railway through the town, and the many estates concerned. This latter difficulty has been removed by the close co-operation of the owners through their surveyors and the Corporation officials. It is illustrated by the directness of many of the main thoroughfares, and particularly with regard to Queen's Road, which involved three estates, and was laid out before the modern idea of "Town Planning" was mooted. The first illustration shows Queen's Road before development with Penny House Farm, the sixteenth century home of the Cunliffes, and, in the distance, the Coppice, part of Peel Park. The railway has always been a difficult obstacle in the laying out of the town, and although several of the bridges have been dealt with, there are others which still require considerable improvement to meet present day conditions.

With regard to the future, lines of proposed roads have been laid down for the undeveloped parts of the Borough which will assist in providing better means of communication to the outside areas. These are in some cases already being worked to by the estate owners, and the proposals will be incorporated in a Town Planning Scheme when the Corporation take advantage of Town Planning legislation to control the development of the remaining portions of the Borough.

QUEEN'S ROAD TO-DAY.

HOUSING.

FROM the time of the incorporation of the Borough, house building kept pace with the requirements of the population to the outbreak of the war, when it practically ceased for three or four years. The general class of house provided during the greater part of this period was of the terrace house type with two and three bedrooms, substantially built, and with well paved front and back streets. These houses were erected at such a reasonable cost that to-day at least 37% of the occupiers are also the owners of the houses they live in. Between 1878 and 1918, there were 5,505 new houses certified for occupation, the greatest number for one year being 339, in 1881, the three hundred again being exceeded in 1889, viz., 310.

After the war, the Corporation was required by the Housing Act of 1919, to survey the housing requirements of the Borough. This showed that there were 3.93 occupiers per house, even after allowing for the men then serving with the forces. Another interesting fact is the small number of the back-to-back type 208, a number which compares very favourably with most industrial towns. As a result of this survey, the Corporation was not required to proceed immediately with a housing scheme, at which time building costs were exorbitant on account of war-time conditions. The Corporation, however, continued to prepare for a building scheme, and purchased the Laneside Estate, in 1921. In July, 1923, the first contract was let for the erection of houses, and the first house was occupied on April 10th, 1924. The whole scheme of 205 houses was completed by January 8th, 1926.

An area of 11½ acres was acquired on the Spring Hill Estate in May, 1925, and 112 houses were erected and completed for occupation by September 30th, 1927.

The houses have been erected at a fairly reasonable cost, and are let at rentals of 7/6 to 9/- per week, plus rates and water charges, which, at the present time, make inclusive totals of 11/2 to 12/11 per week.

The Corporation also put into operation the powers given by the Housing Act of 1923, to assist private house building by means of a subsidy for each house erected to certain conditions.

Under the Small Dwellings Acquisition Acts, the Corporation advance loans on Mortgage for constructing or acquiring houses for the applicant's occupation. The repayment of these loans is spread over a period of 20 years, and quarterly instalments of principal and interest are accepted. To the 31st March, 1928, there had been advanced for this purpose, £8,670.

LANESIDE HOUSING SCHEME.

These facilities stimulated house-building so that a further 300 houses have been built during this period, which makes a total of 6,122 houses erected and certified during the fifty years since the incorporation of the Borough.

A remarkable feature of the housing problem to-day is that with 11,851 houses for an estimated population of 43, 190, the number of occupiers per house has decreased from about five in 1878, to 3.64 at the present time.

The post-war type of house works out at about 16 per acre, as against about 25 to 30 per acre of the general pre-war type of terrace house. It is well planned and convenient from the labour saving point of view; every house being provided with a bath, modern fittings, and having improved sanitary arrangements.

The number of owner-occupier houses at the present time is approximately 4,300.

ALLOTMENTS.

THE provision of permanent allotments was catered for by the Corporation acquiring Miller Fold, Brox, Gallows Hall, Ley and Shoe Mill, and Miry Lane Farms, in 1908. These comprise a total area of 130 acres, 0 roods, 18 poles, and at the present time there are 61 acres, 1 rood, 29 poles taken up for allotments at Miller Fold, Brox, and Ley Farms, the remainder being in agricultural occupation. It is also probable that a portion of the Hollins Farm Estate will be set apart for this purpose.

HEALTH.

IN reviewing the items of progress since the Borough was incorporated 50 years ago, nothing gives one greater pleasure than to recount the eminent progress of our latest Ante-Natal endeavours during the present year. The possibilities of extending this work have been furthered by the opening of the Rough Lee Maternity Home, where a room is set apart for the carrying on of this work every Friday morning from 10-0 to 12-0. All expectant mothers within the Borough are invited to attend and take advantage of these meetings. That the Ante-Natal Clinic should progress so well speaks volumes for the intelligence and far-sightedness of the mothers of the Borough. There is no department in municipal life which so well expresses good government, both on the part of the governors and the governed, than capable and adequate provisions for such work. The estimated cost for the present year is £927.

In the report for the year 1891, of Dr. Thos. Milne (M.O.H.), he remarks: "The year throughout was cold and wet, the summer being particularly dreary." These words would apply to some years since that time, though not to all. The population then was 38,603. One of his tables shews that 1882 was a ghastly year as regards scarlet fever, no fewer than 138 deaths being due to that disease, and in the year 1889, 141 deaths are recorded as being due to measles. Other parts of his reports deal incidentally with the excellent work then being carried out with regard to the sewers and drains of the Borough, which formed a substantial foundation for better results.

Those who are interested can find in the Borough Surveyor's Office or the Public Library, a complete survey of all the streams which go to make up the River Hyndburn. One stream called Pleck Brook, comes down from above Moleside End and finally runs under Whalley Road into the River Hyndburn. Another stream, named Hag Brook, begins in the neighbourhood of Hameldon, and just above Broad Oak Works it joins with the Warmden Clough Brook which rises in Black Moss. These united streams join with the Worsley Brook, which has its rise in the neighbourhood of Black Moss, underneath Broad Oak Works. They pass under Manchester Road, down Grange Lane, where they are joined on the left bank by a stream which comes down Priestley Clough from Baxenden, and form the River Hyndburn. This latter runs under the Market Hall, along Pleck Meadows, over the waterfall on the east side of Bull Bridge, thence along Hyndburn Road to the Borough Boundary, on through Dunkenhalgh, under the Hyndburn Bridge, Whalley Road (Clayton-le-Moors), finally to join with the Calder. This great survey, which must have taken a lot of time and labour, shews in red, all the sources of contamination and otherwise to which the streams were exposed. The taking out of these impurities, and the diverting of them to a proper sewage scheme was a labour of fundamental importance for the future health of the area. The number of openings was considerably over 400, and it must be left to the imagination to visualize the amount of work that had to be done to get this mass of offence turned into right channels; sewage to go to the drains and only water into the river bed.

In the year 1892, Dr. Monaghan, the then M.O.H., recommended to the Council the provision of destructors for the cremation of household refuse, etc. Also, that steps be taken to lessen the pollution of the river and water courses by trade refuse, and that the work of altering more primitive methods to the water-carriage system be continued on a larger scale. In the same report he refers to the contamination of the air by the black smoke from the mill and workshop chimneys, and recommended the authorities to take more energetic measures for the abatement of this nuisance. In 1893, he makes strong recommendation for special attention to be paid to the more efficient flushing of the sewers: these have since been made self-cleansing. In 1894, which all over the country was a phenomenal one for good health statistics, he alludes to the very low infant mortality of 122 per 1,000 births. Last year (1927), our corresponding figure was 61 per 1,000 births; exactly half of what the doctor was more than proud of them. In 1895, he complains about the nuisance caused by waste steam and hot water from factory boilers passing into the sewers likely to cause fermentative changes in the sewage. His recommendations in the year 1896 repeat what he had said in previous years, but add the advisability of constructing a common lodging house by the authority to be under municipal control.

During the last thirty years an enormous amount of work has been done, some quite good, some very bad, and much left undone. The best work has been done during more recent years in connexion with Infant Welfare. The report for the year 1899, shews the Infant Mortality of Accrington to be about 179 per thousand; Clayton-Le-Moors, 203; Oswaldtwistle, 204; England and Wales, 163. In addition to this, the School Medical Service has come, the institution of a Clinic for minor ailments, the provision of treatment for more formidable ailments, arrangements for the isolation of infectious diseases where thought advisable, and the institution of Chaigeley Manor, to which reference is made later. The cost of the School Medical Service for the current year is estimated at £850. Amongst the bad work must be reckoned the wholesale adoption of the waste water closet: though it is now thirteen years since a so-called "waste water closet" was constructed in the borough. The work which might have been done to the great advantage of the health of the borough was the paving of the bed of the River Hyndburn.

Casting one's eyes over the items of progress which have been undertaken since these earlier years of the borough's incorporation, the first of note is the scheme for the isolation of infectious diseases. A Smallpox Hospital for this particular disease alone was erected within the borough in 1903 at a cost of £1,300. It was useful in an epidemic during the year 1903, when over 86 cases were treated there. At different times meetings have been held with the adjoining authorities of Church, Clayton-Le-Moors, and Oswaldtwistle, to discuss schemes for the erection of a hospital for infectious diseases for the whole area, but the discussions never developed into building schemes. There has, however, always been (certainly during recent years), adequate arrangement for the isolation of these cases when necessary.

The School Medical Service, which came into existence in the year 1913, has, from a small beginning, when the authorities were content simply to notify parents or guardians of any defect found, now developed schemes for the carrying out of treatment. Arrangements have been made for treatment at Victoria Hospital (under the care of a specialist), of all diseases of the throat, nose and ears, and a special Clinic is held for defects of vision. During the present year a whole time dentist has been appointed, and for some years now a Clinic for the treatment of minor ailments has been open for the children every morning in the week.

For the last nine years, use has been made of Chaigeley Manor, which is situated near Stonyhurst, for the purpose of a Convalescent Home for the school children of the district. During the war, the Manor was used as an Auxiliary Hospital, afterwards it was loaned for the purpose of a Convalescent Home by the Co-operative Wholesale Society, to a Committee representing this district. During the present year the Manor has come into the possession of this Committee, having been purchased outright from the Co-operative Wholesale Society. The Mayor of the Borough is its President and the School Medical Officer has, right from its beginning, acted as Honorary Medical Officer. The school children go down for periods of three weeks, which period may be extended in suitable cases on the recommendation of the School Medical Officer. Nearly 1,000 children have been down for recuperation since the home was devoted to this purpose.

The Infants are looked after at a special clinic on Thursday afternoon, but they may also be brought any morning of the week for inspection and advice, so that, through the Maternity Home, the Infant Welfare Clinic, the care of children under school age, and throughout their school life, the physical well-being of the children of the Borough is quite carefully provided for. This department is estimated to cost £583, in 1928-29. During the current year the town has joined a scheme designed by the Lancashire County Council for dealing with children requiring orthopaedic treatment. This branch of surgery deals with the art of curing deformities of the body, especially in childhood. No one would begrudge what is spent on this effort to remove, if possible, if not, to mitigate the distress of children so circumstanced. For the present a specialist visits the Clinic at Rishton once a month, and a special orthopaedic nurse at other times.

MATERNITY HOME, ROUGH LEE.

THE POLICE.

THE date when the first regularly appointed Police Force came into being in Accrington is involved in obscurity, but at a Vestry meeting, held in Accrington on the 20th September, 1821, it was decided that in future the Constables of the said town be ordered to attend Church every Sunday, regularly, assist the Churchwardens in the execution of their office. At the same meeting, it was directed that Common Begging be put a stop to, and to accomplish this, the meeting ordered that James Barnes and his son, if agreeable to them, be appointed Constables for the purpose of carrying before the Magistrates all Vagrants found begging, and the town agreed to remunerate them for their trouble.

A select Vestry, for the management of the Poor, was appointed on the 2nd January, 1827, signed by John Hopwood, Magistrate, consisting of Robert Peel, Benjamin Wilson, James Wilson, George Pickup, John Pilling Worsley, John Hargreaves, Edmund Peel, James Worsley and William Walmsley, 10 persons in all, and it is thought that this was the first select Vestry appointed for the Poor in New Accrington.

At a Vestry meeting, held on the 14th June, 1827, called for the purpose of taking into consideration the desirability of having a Deputy Chief Constable for the townships of Old and New Accrington, it was agreed that a Deputy Chief Constable be appointed for the above townships, and that he have £10 0s. 0d., per annum, which sum is to be paid by the townships in the proportion per £ of 14/7 from New Accrington, and 5/5 from Old Accrington.

At a second meeting held on the 21st June, 1827, it was resolved that Edmund Kenyon appointed at the salary above mentioned, so long as his conduct shall be approved of, and that such salary shall be paid by the two townships on the rates just stated.
Kenyon did not reign very long, for at a meeting held on the 5th May, 1828, it was unanimously agreed that Joseph Booth be appointed Deputy Constable for the townships of Old and New Accrington for the year ensuing, at the rate of £10 0s. 0d. per annum, which amount was increased to £15, in May, 1836.

It is reported that on the 24th March, 1840, Policemen arrived in Accrington at 3-3 in the afternoon, and it is thought that this was the first introduction of regular Policemen of this Borough. (This last item of information has been obtained from the diary of Mr. Thomas Swindles, who occupied the position of School Master at Baxenden.)

The Public Library contains the original of a memorial presented to Her Majesty's Justices of the Peace, sitting in Petty Session in the Court Room in Accrington, shewing that "Whereas in the year of our Lord one-thousand eight-hundred and twenty-eight, a complete set of measures, weights, and scales, of the standard of the Imperial Exchequer, was subscribed for by the shopkeepers and others in the townships of Old and New Accrington, aforesaid, for the purpose of having their own weights and measures adjusted thereby, and whereas the office of Inspector of Weights and Measures for the said townships has since that time been held by Joseph Booth, by appointment of two of His late Majesty's Justices of the Peace, and whereas by reason of age and infirmities the said Joseph Booth is now incapable of properly discharging the duties of the said office. We, therefore, most respectfully request that you will be pleased to appoint a disinterested and respectable householder of Accrington to the above office with full powers for the proper and efficient discharge of all its duties. May 1st, 1849." The memorial was signed by 107 shopkeepers and residents of the townships. One signature it is that of the late William Entwisle, one of the first members of the Council of the Borough and a Justice of the Peace.

At the time that Accrington was made a Borough, fifty years ago, it was an Inspectors' station, attached to the Blackburn Lower Division of the County, the Head-quarters of which was Burnley. The Superintendent was Mr. Wright, and the Inspector-in-charge, James Eatough. There were three Sergeants and sixteen Constables for the town; amongst the latter was the late James Beattie who was a plain-clothes Constable. The present Chief Constable came to Accrington at the time of the election of the first Town Council.

At that time, the whole of North-East Lancashire was passing through the throes of a great industrial upheaval, namely-the Great

Cotton Strike of 1878. Serious disturbances occurred all over the area. The Military-horse and foot-were stationed in every town. Serious rioting took place and many were seriously injured. Large numbers of the rioters were proceeded against and committed to Lancaster Assizes where they were brought up for trial before Lord Coleridge-the Lord Chief Justice of England.

When the Force was formed on the 1st January, 1883, it consisted of thirty-two men, all told-one Chief Constable, one Inspector, one Detective Sergeant, three Sergeants, one Sergeant-Clerk, and twenty-five Constables. The strength of the Force now is fifty one Chief Constable, three Inspectors, one Detective Sergeant, four Sergeants, and forty-one Constables.

Accrington's first Chief Constable, Mr. Joseph Walker, had only a short time in office, for in less than two years from his appointment he was taken seriously ill and died on the 17th December, 1884. Mr. Beattie was appointed his successor and held office until 1903, when he retired on pension owing to ill-health, and the present Chief Constable was appointed.

Quite a number of Labour Disputes have taken place during the fifty years, but no serious disturbance has occurred. The Criminal Statistics of Accrington will bear most favourable comparison with towns of a similar size.

The Sunday Schools, which are highly organized in Accrington, can be heartily congratulated on the part they have played in keeping crime down, and cordial relations have always existed between those responsible for Law and Order and the general public.

LICENSING. The earliest reference to a licensed house in the town is in 1642, when "there was a Bay Horse Hotel, probably on the site of the present building," (Crossley). Further reference is to be found to the "Black Bull," and it is evident there were at least two ale-houses for the use of the community in the middle of the seventeenth century, and probably much earlier. In 1883 (the earliest figures available), the number of licensed houses in the town was 137, of which number 39 were either "off" or "wholesale." In 1927-

28, the number had been reduced to 103, of which 30 were "off" license holders. Against this reduction must be placed the addition of 21 clubs registered under the Licensing (Consolidation) Act, 1910.

The cost of the maintenance of the Police force during the year 1883, was £2,990. The receipts amounted to £1,137, of which amount £1,052 was received as Government Grant. In 1927-28, the expenditure was £15,301, which was covered as follows-Grant, £7,066; other receipts, £1,292; income from rates, £6,943.

EDUCATION.

"I am convinced that nothing is more essential to National prosperity and happiness than Education. A true education would transform our National life in a generation." His Majesty the King.

ACCRINGTON SCHOOLS IN THE EARLY PART OF THE 19TH CENTURY.

The following information, based upon the Parliamentary Inquiry of 1833, concerning the schools in every parish in England, is interesting:

ACCRINGTON NEW. (Part of Whalley Parish). Population, 4,960.

One Endowed School with	140 boys	70 girls
Five other Schools (dating 1823 to 1833)	68 boys	139 girls
Total	208 boys	209 girls

NATIONAL SCHOOL, CHURCH STREET.

In the Non-Endowed Schools, the children were educated at the expense of their parents.

In addition to these daily schools there were five Sunday Schools (three Church of England, one Baptist, one New Jersualem) attended by 607 males and 544 females.

ACCRINGTON OLD. (Chapelry: Population, 1,323).
Had one Daily School (commenced 1826) of 51 boys and 6 girls, whose instruction was paid for by their parents. There were also two Sunday Schools one Wesleyan and one Baptist, attended by 285 males and 254 females. Both had Lending Libraries attached.

INFANT STREET SCHOOL.

The following remarks from the Report refer to Lancashire as a whole:

"In 102 Schools the children leave at seven years of age. In most of the Infants' Schools the children commenced at two years of age, and at Lancaster and Ormskirk at 18 months."

Unlike many towns, Accrington had no old foundation Grammar School such as were established in the Tudor Period. Since the middle of the nineteenth century, however, it has had a vigorous system of Primary Schools, which were established by the various religious denominations. The following table shows the system of Elementary Schools in 1845:

	Average Attendance.
St. James' National School	190
St. James' Infant School	70
Christ Church School	160
New Jerusalem School	170
Baptist School	135
Methodist School	35
Broad Oak Works School	80
Total	840
To these may be added Private and Dame Schools	131

The National School, Church Street, erected in 1816, by public subscription, was opened as a Sunday School that year (August 18th), by the historian of Whalley (Dr. Whitaker). It was opened as a Day School in June, 1824, and used as such until the completion of the new School in Cannon Street, in 1896.

The Foundation Stone of Infant Street School was laid by Mrs. John Hargreaves, on the 18th May, 1840.

Of the later Private Schools the most notable were Dr. Bayley's in Whalley Road, known as Bayley's Academy, and that of Mr. F. N. Haywood (afterwards Alderman and Mayor of the Borough). The number of scholars enrolled in all schools must have been (say) 1,300-one scholar to every six or seven of the population, estimating

SCHOOL COURT, CHURCH STREET, SHOWING THE GABLE
END OF THE NATIONAL SCHOOL.

the inhabitants in 1850 to number 8,300. In 1871, the year following the great Education Act of 1870, which authorized the establishment of School Boards, the Day School scholars numbered:

Church of England   1256

Nonconformist 1579
Roman Catholic 160
Total 2995

INTERIOR OF HAYWOOD'S SCHOOL.

Accrington at no time established a School Board, the Managers of Voluntary Schools having to rely for the finances of their Schools upon Government Grants, school fees (until these were partially abolished in 1891, and finally by the Education Act of 1918) and voluntary contributions. The Education Act of 1902 allowed the Voluntary Schools to be aided from the rates, as in the case of the Schools provided by the Town Council, which now became the Local Education Authority. An Education Committee was constituted in 1903, and with the increased financial resources available and a realization of the wider possibilities for elementary education opened out by the Act, they proceeded on a policy of the gradual replacement of the old Voluntary Schools which had done their work so nobly and well under great difficulties. Thus the following new Council Schools were established within a short space of time:

Spring Hill (with its Infants' Department in Hannah Street) acquired by purchase	1905
Hyndburn Park, erected	1906
Woodnook, erected	1909
Peel Park, erected	1910
Total accommodation	3,246 places.

What handsome structures are these! And they were very wisely fitted up with facilities for Practical Work for both boys and girls.

The following Voluntary or Non-Provided Schools have been closed since 1902:

Christ Church National	29th August, 1909
Hargreaves Street (New Jerusalem)	28th February, 1917
Woodnook Baptist	29th August, 1900
Antley Wesleyan	26th August, 1906
Cambridge Street Wesleyan	August, 1910
Union Street Wesleyan	26th August, 1906

but no less than eleven Non-Provided Schools with 4,967 places still flourish alongside the Council Schools, the system established by the 1902 Act being known as the "Dual System."

The Education Act of 1918 (the "Fisher" Act), opened up new vistas of progress for educational enthusiasts, for all forms of education were to be encouraged. Unfortunately, some of the splendid ideals indicated in the Act have been hitherto unattainable owing to the financial state of the country. Yet much has been done. Advanced instruction for scholars of 11 years and upwards has been provided by the establishment of a Central School at Hyndburn Park with accommodation for 360 scholars. At the other end of the scale provision has been made for the mentally backward by means of a special class under a well-qualified teacher.

The School Medical Service, established under the Administrative Provisions Act of 1907, has been developed along sound lines, and is greatly appreciated by the parents and children. The physical well-being of the children is safeguarded by a regular system of medical inspection every child is examined three times during its school life-a daily Minor Ailments Clinic, dental inspection and treatment at the new Dental Clinic, examination of eyes, ears, nose, and throat, by a Specialist, with treatment where necessary at our excellent Victoria Hospital. A scheme has this year, been established for the treatment of crippling defects, whilst a new Open Air School for delicate children will shortly be erected at Rough Lee, so that it will be readily seen how comprehensive is this splendid recent feature of school life.

JAMES FENWICK, FOR SOME TWENTY YEARS SCHOOL ATTENDANCE OFFICER, WAS ASSOCIATED AS A LOCAL PREACHER WITH THE PARTICULAR BAPTISTS. HE DIED IN 1895.

There is also a fully equipped Lending Library Service in each school for children in Standards III and IV, worked in conjunction with the Public Library Department and the teachers. Last year 38,026 volumes were issued. Children in the upper standards secure their books for home reading from the Public Library, with which there is complete co-operation.

What of the future of Elementary Education in the Borough? The true line of development seems to be in the establishment of Junior (or Infants' and junior,) Schools up to the age of 11 plus, and then advanced and practical instruction for all normal children over 11 years in selective and non-selective or Senior Schools as recommended in the famous Hadow Report of 1926, and confirmed by the Board of Education.

HIGHER EDUCATION.

The genesis of the higher education of the people is to be found in the establishment of that famous Accrington institution the Mechanics' Institution which was founded in 1845. Started in Blackburn Road with a News Room, Library, occasional Lectures and Entertainments, it had, as its object, the moral and intellectual improvement of the people. Evening Classes were started and a professional teacher was engaged: the curriculum in these early days (1856) did not extend beyond Reading, Writing, Arithmetic (the three R's) and Grammar. In 1859, the Mechanics' Institution removed from No. 18 Blackburn Road, to the Peel Institution, the handsome structure-now the Town Hall which was built as a Memorial to the great Sir Robert Peel. The Cotton Famine lasting from 1862 to 1866, inflicted severe losses and privation on the inhabitants of the town, who, however, revealed high qualities of endurance, independence, and mutual helpfulness, the results of their training in thrift, education, and religion.

By 1876, the Library of the Institution contained 4,300 volumes, the Evening Continuation Classes had an average attendance of 80 or 90, and the first Government Grant of £15 18s. 6d., had been received in 1873. Science Classes had been started in 1858, Practical Chemistry being taught "in the Laboratory over the Fire Engine

Station" The following table for 1877-78, shows the great popularity of the Science and Art Classes:

SCIENCE.

	Students.
Mathematics	40
Acoustics, Light, and Heat	30
Animal Physiology	23
Machine Construction, etc.	20
Geology	16
Magnetism and Electricity	70
Inorganic Chemistry	50
Practical Chemistry	30
Steam	8

ART.

Freehand Drawing	40
Geometry	10
Model Drawing	22
Perspective Drawing	3

The work of the Education Committee of the Accrington and Church Industrial Co-operative Society is worthy of note. In 1878 the Society voted for educational purposes the sum of £274; from 1863 to 1878, £2,304 was spent in promoting educational objects; its Evening School had 190 scholars on roll, and its Science Classes, which included one for the study of Agriculture (the first in the town), reported 60 students, by whom 11 Government prizes were taken in one year.

In 1878, the Mechanics' Institution moved to Willow House, which, considerably enlarged, became known as the Mechanics' Institution. Its Elementary Evening Classes continued to be held for some years longer, in addition to which there were classes in French, German, Music, and Technical Subjects. Striking successes in National competitions were gained by Science students. For two years a Day Higher Grade School was also conducted, but was abandoned in 1887. Cotton Weaving was added as a subject of instruction, whilst the Art Department became exceedingly popular.

A notable experiment in the technical and scientific training of apprentices was undertaken by Messrs. Howard and Bullough, the great local firm of textile machinery manufacturers. Classes were started at the Works in 1882, and by 1884 they had obtained recognition by the Science and Art Department, South Kensington. A large and handsome room, entered from Richmond Hill Street, was fitted up (the decorations alone costing over £1,000), and furnished with the best possible apparatus and machinery. The Science and Technical Courses included mathematics, magnetism and electricity, applied mechanics, machine construction and drawing, and cotton spinning. All apprentices were obliged to attend the School until they were 21 years of age. In one year there were 374 Science and 62 Technical Students, whilst there were 346 scholars in the Continuation School, which provided continued elementary education. The School continued until 1903, when the firm, with their usual generosity, handed over the desks, fittings, apparatus and machinery, to the Municipal Technical School.

MECHANICS' INSTITUTION AND WILLOW HOUSE.

PEEL PARK COUNCIL SCHOOL.
Photo by Jones.

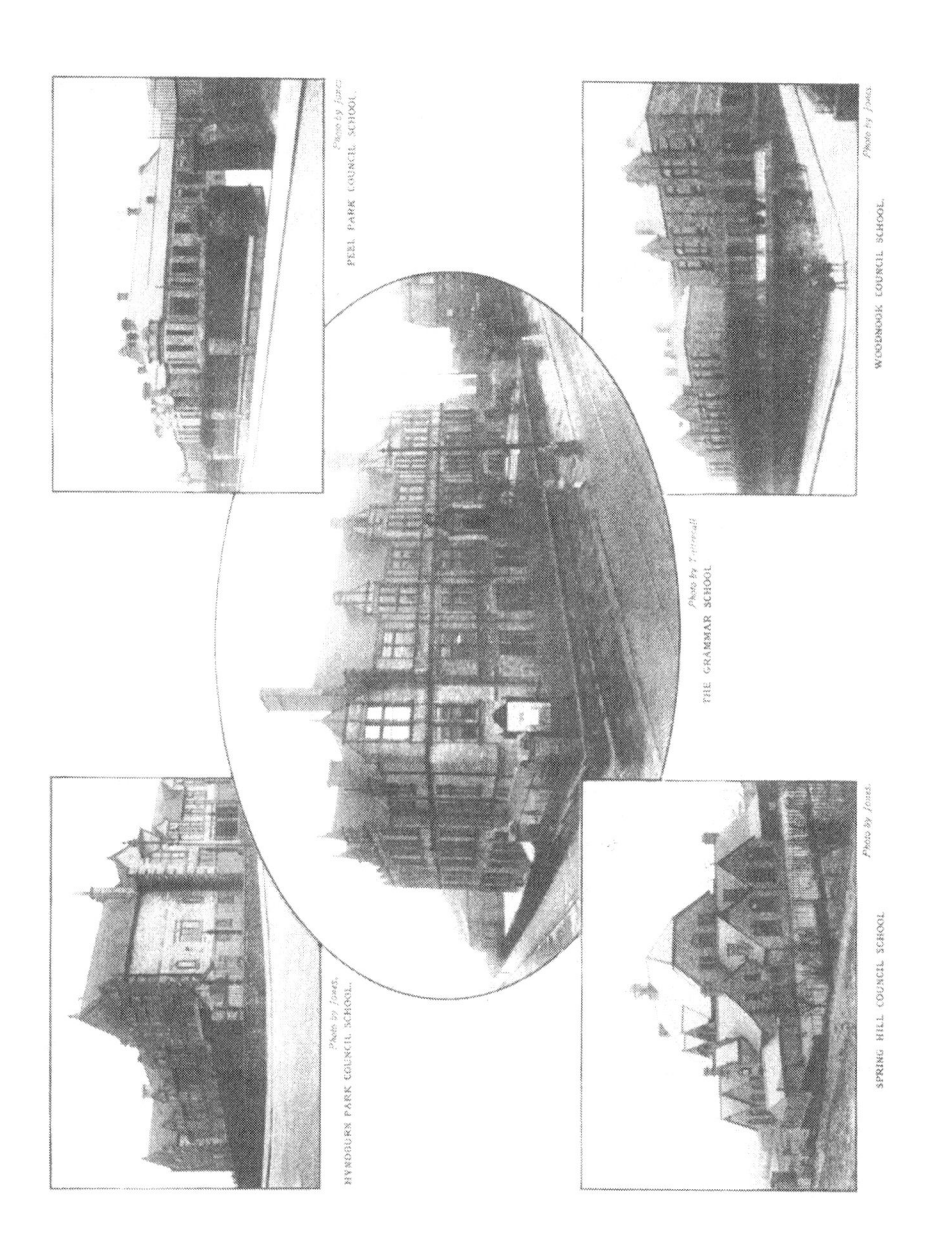

WOODNOOK COUNCIL SCHOOL.
Photo by Jones.

THE GRAMMAR SCHOOL
Photo by Greenwell.

HYNDBURN PARK COUNCIL SCHOOL.
Photo by Jones.

SPRING HILL COUNCIL SCHOOL
Photo by Jones.

With the handing over of their classes by the Mechanics' Institution, which had now taken on a purely social and recreative character, to the Technical Instruction Committee of the Town Council in 1893, begins the history of modern higher education in the Borough. The Town Council built the handsome three-storey structure in Blackburn Road as a Technical School in 1895. Started as an Organized Science School with 62 pupils of both sexes, the Day Department gradually developed into a Secondary School and Pupil Teachers' Centre. The Evening Department provided instruction for large numbers, in Science, technological and commercial subjects, whilst the Day and Evening Art School also flourished, producing some notable students and craftsmen. The Day Secondary School is now known as the Grammar School, the whole administration of Higher Education passing to the County Council by the Education Act of 1902. The management, however, is in the hands of the Accrington Higher Education Committee, who act as the Governors of the School.

The buildings were considerably enlarged in 1906, whilst in 1926, a notable addition was the School of Engineering in College Street. The following figures give an indication of the volume of Higher Education work proceeding at the present time: in the Autumn Term, 1927, the Grammar School had 546 pupils; the Technical School, 551 students; the Art School, 216; the four Evening Continuation Schools, 417. The following Courses were provided at the Technical School: Engineering, Cotton Spinning, Cotton Weaving, Building Construction, Plumbing, Chemistry, Commerce, Music, Dressmaking, Millinery, and Cookery.

In connexion with educational administration in the Borough, two names stand out with special prominence: Alderman J. W. Cunliffe, Chairman of the Technical Instruction Committee and Education Committee for a total period of eighteen years, and Alderman Langham, formerly the well-known Head Master of Willow Street Baptist School, who was Chairman from 1910 until 1922. These gentlemen have evinced in their work, public spirit and ability of the highest order, and have indelibly stamped their impress on Education in the Borough.

Much remains for future development, but the foundations have been well and truly laid, and our Borough may well be proud of the achievements of the last fifty years. With an enlightened administration, with a loyal and devoted body of teachers such as the Borough possesses, with children quick to respond to spiritual, moral, and intellectual influences, the Borough may confidently look forward to a still higher standard of life and citizenship.

RETROSPECT.

1800 to 1832.	Children of 7 years and upwards working 12 hours per day, 6 days per week.
1833 to 1843.	Children over 8 working 9 hours per day, and when not working to be educated.
1844 to 1870.	Children under 13 to work 6½ hours per day and attend school 2 to 3½ hours per day.
1870.	Provision of Schools sufficient for all children made compulsory.
1874.	Children under 10 debarred from factories.
1876.	Attendance at School made compulsory.
1891.	Children under 12 debarred from factories, and education made free.
1903.	All children 5 to 12 to attend School.
1928.	All children from 5 to 14 attend school, full time. Many continue at the Grammar School until the age of 18 for Advanced Courses.

THE PUBLIC LIBRARY.

THERE are evidences of early efforts in the provision of literature for the reading public of Accrington. The earliest we have any note of is one which was apparently in the care of the incumbent of the parish, and its only record a book label in the library's possession. This may have been the fore-runner (?) of the "library founded some years ago by the late Mrs. Benjamin Hargreaves for the benefit of the working-men of Accrington, and lately added to by a bequest (£100) of the same lady" (St. James's Parish Magazine, October, 1868). This library was "open to all above the age of 18, who shall produce a recommendation and guarantee from two ratepayers."

The town also possessed a Subscription Library "formed at a shop in Bank Street, with Mr, Altham as librarian": it was called "The Institution." This library "was afterwards transferred to Mr. Holt's, Abbey Street." On his removal it was located above his shop at 31 Blackburn Road. This was later handed over as a gift to what eventually became the Accrington Mechanics' Institution, but was at first known as the Accrington Subscription Library: the date of its inception was April 1th, 1845. It was established "with a view to afford increased facilities for moral and intellectual improvement." The first president was Mr. Benjamin Hargreaves, the first directors being elected on April 18th, the same year. In a catalogue of the books, printed by William Hutchinson in 1845, the entries are made according to size-folios, quartos, etc., and the copy in the possession of the library is of interest from the manuscript notes inserted "New Books to come from Library, London, Jane Eyre, 3 vols. Mary Barton, or, Manchester Life, 2 vols.," etc.

The title of the Institution was changed to its present one in 1851. It was the main source of the supply of literature for many years, but in 1875, an attempt was made to establish a public library in Accrington. A petition was presented to the Local Board of Health, and a meeting of ratepayers was held in the Peel Institution on July 24th, 1875, in order to determine whether the Public Libraries Acts should or should not be adopted. The Peel Institution at that time belonged to the town, and the question arose primarily upon an application of the Directors of the Mechanics' Institution for a renewal of their lease of a portion of the building. The meeting was chiefly composed of members of the Institution, and the resolution to adopt the Acts was defeated by a very large majority. In 1887, the members of the Mechanics' Institution met to consider handing over the charge of the Institution, its Library, and Classes, to the care of the town, but this proposal was defeated. The movement towards the establishment of a Public Library took definite shape in 1899 when, on the 5th June, the Public Libraries Acts were unanimously adopted by the Town Council, and a Committee appointed, of which the late Mr. James Cunliffe, J.P., was the first Chairman. The bequest of £500 by Mr. John E. Stansfield, conditional upon steps being taken within twelve months to establish a library, probably expedited matters. A portion of the present Mechanics' Institution, with an entrance from Willow Street, was rented as a Lending Department, the first book being issued on the 9th April, 1901. A Subscription List for the purchase of the initial stock of books realized the sum of £738 5s. 10d., and the Library was opened with 6,009 volumes. Accommodation for Reading Room purposes was found in the Market Hall the gallery along the east side being used as a general Reading Room, and part of the front gallery, now used as the Tramways Department Offices, as a Ladies' Reading Room.

These conditions with their attendant disabilities, continued until January, 1908, when the present building, the gift of Mr. Andrew Carnegie, was opened. The cost of the building and fittings, erected on the plans of the Borough Engineer (Mr. W. J. Newton) was £9,500. Again, the Mechanics' Institution came to the help of the town, not only granting the site of the present library containing in all an area of 1.438 square yards, but their books also. What was known as Willow House, where the Mechanics' Library was housed, was demolished to make way for the building now used for Public Library purposes; the Stansfield bequest being used to redeem the ground rent.

The Library now contains 33,695 volumes, exclusive of some 400 pamphlets and documents. Its growth in popularity may best be tested by figures. The issue of books for home reading in 1901-02, totalled 74,680; in 1911-12, 105,549; in 1921-22, 151,215; and in 1927-28, 243,163. The policy of the Committee of recent years, has been to keep the library well stocked with new books, and whilst this has meant an increase in the cost of the service, the results have fully justified their action. Since the issue of the first book in 1901, 4,234,183 volumes have been circulated in the town. The library is particularly strong in local literature (i.e., Lancashire in general, and Accrington in particular), and contains over 1,700 books and pamphlets of local interest. Music is also well represented, the stock in this section numbering 1,100 volumes. There are, too, excellent facilities for students engaged in local industries. In all it is estimated that something like 2,000 people use the building daily: the cost per head of the population per annum being 1s. 3.4d. In 1901-02, the expenditure on library service was £799, in 1927-28, £2,809 18s. 2d. The figures given indicate that the library is being increasingly used by the community, and is keeping pace locally with the manifest advance nationally in the appreciation of the services possible in a public library.

THE PUBLIC LIBRARY.

EARLY MANUSCRIPTS AND PRINTED BOOKS.

The Public Library contains many old manuscripts, documents, and deeds relating to the district; the earliest is really an undated copy and relates to Grindleton in the year 1587, whereby it appears there was not sufficient accommodation for the grazing of cattle in the village, and the inhabitants received Her Majesty's permission to use part of Grindleton Moor.

The earliest relating to the Halmot Court of the Manor of Accrington is in the reign of King James the First. The early manuscripts also include the New Accrington Survey Book of 1790, in which the names of the owners and tenants, and the acreage and value are set out. This volume is of further interest from the fact that it contains, in a different handwriting, a valuation of Broad Oak Print Works, July 1st, 1822, almost at the time illustrated herein. The valuation, including certain cottages, is given as £258 11s. 10¼d. A second survey, in excellent condition, gives a "Valuation of the New Hold of Accrington made by Wm. Woodcock of Manchester, May 26th, 1829," These two volumes give valuable details of ownership in the town in the late eighteenth and early nineteenth centuries. Another manuscript volume is an old mill account book lettered on the outside, as near as one can tell, "The Miscellany of R. Riley and E. Riley." The earliest dates in it refer to January, 1792, and it appears to be a record of yarn given to the weavers, and of the amount paid for the finished material. A name appears at the top of each page, and occasionally an address. One page is here reproduced in the hope that someone may be able to elucidate its use more certainly.

It would be of interest to ascertain definitely the precise date of the first book bearing an Accrington imprint. The earliest in the Library is "A collection of psalms and hymns sung at Church Kirk, Accrington: printed by R. J. Salter, stationer and bookbinder," There is no date of publication, but an ownership mark "Ellen Whewell Book, January 4th, 1829," proves that its latest date of printing must have been 1828. How much earlier one cannot tell. It is not, of course, safe to assume that the book was actually printed in the town: it bears the marks of hand-press and not machine press work, which is something in favour of local production.

PAGE FROM AN OLD MILL RECORD OF 1792-3.

The book may actually have been printed at Manchester, but it is the earliest so far discovered bearing the imprint of Accrington. R. J. Salter is the earliest known Accrington printer. A copy of a sheet containing a notice of two sermons to be preached in the Baptist Chapel, Accrington, on Sunday, May 21st, 1815, and setting out the hymns to be sung thereat, was printed at Blackburn. It hardly seems likely to have been printed there if there had been anyone in the town at that time capable of doing the work. It would be interesting to know of any books printed prior to 1828.

ELECTRICAL ENGINEERING DEPARTMENT.

ACCRINGTON Electricity Works, situated on the banks of the Hyndburn, were founded in 1900, electricity being first supplied on November 9th, of that year. In the intervening years the works have been completely reconstructed, and scarcely a vestige of the original buildings or plant remain in this, the Jubilee Year.

In the initial year, the number of consumers was but 112, and the length of mains 3½ miles. To-day, there radiates from the works 80 miles of mains, penetrating every corner of the town and transmitting light and power to the adjoining townships of Oswaldtwistle, Church, Clayton-le-Moors, Altham, Rishton, and to the Borough of Haslingden, to over 5,000 consumers. The following table gives particulars of the supply in the area:

District	Miles of Mains	No. of Consumers	Power	Lighting	Domestic use	Total Units Sold
Accrington	54.06	4,173	11,092,931	1,159,725	1,166,232	12,418,888
Church	6.34	292	302,585	65,795	45,827	414,207
Clayton-le-Moors	8.71	507	394,918	92,997	116,408	604,323
Altham	4.24	72	1,373,668	5,696	34,465	1,413,829
Oswald-twistle	7.69	354	165,057	97,512	70,109	332,678
Haslingden Bulk Supply	-	-	-	-	-	1,703,848

The original plant consisted of three high speed steam engines of 90 h.p., and the capacity of the plant was 168 kilowatts. The capital expenditure was £36,900; the number of units sold being 100,000; and the average price received per unit, 3.88d.

The demand constantly increased as the prices charged diminished, and additions to plant were: made at frequent intervals, until in 1906, it had been enlarged to a capacity of 888 kilowatts; five times the original capacity. The firm of Howard and Bullough became customers of the town for electricity, and in 1907-8, another 1,000 kilowatts plant was added.

The year 1908, brought another definite stage in the rapid growth of the works, for in August of that year the plant was required to furnish the motive power for the town's tramway system. In that year the number of consumers had grown to 468, and the average price had fallen to 1.37d. per unit.

USE BY OUTSIDE AUTHORITIES. In 1910, the mains were extended into the township of Church, and in 1911, Clayton-le-Moors and Altham, under agreements made between the respective local government authorities. The mains were subsequently extended to Rishton, to supply current to the Rishton Paper Works, which are on the fringe of the boundary.

Haslingden Town Council, after fully investigating the question of embarking upon the manufacture of electricity for the town, decided that the most economical course to adopt was to take a supply from Accrington Corporation and since then Accrington has supplied Haslingden with electricity in bulk, for distribution by the neighbouring authority.

In 1922, the Electricity Commissioners, a body set up to centralize the production and distribution of electricity throughout the country, granted the Corporation power to supply electricity to the township of Oswaldtwistle, and despite the low price of gas in that area, the number of electricity consumers has steadily advanced.

FURTHER EXTENSIONS. In 1912-13, the plant was extended to 3,388 kilowatts, a gas engine plant being installed in that year. This subsequently failed to realize expectations, and was gradually superseded. In 1914-15, Accrington Corporation were selling electricity at an average price of .966 of a penny per unit, but a loss of £3,000 was sustained, though the output reached 6,000,000 units.

The outbreak of the war was followed by increased prices of all commodities, and it was in that difficult period (1916), the first 2,000 kilowatt steam turbine, generating electricity at 6,600 volts, was installed.

POST-WAR PROGRESS. In 1920, the boom trade period, the output reached 8,962,000 units, and the number of consumers increased to 2,163, despite the then charge of 2d. per unit, increased to 2.4d. in 1921, to recoup the losses incurred during the period of fluctuating costs.

In the six following years, the demand increased by leaps and bounds, the number of consumers increasing to over 5,000. During the same period, the average price was reduced to 1.48d., a price which compares favourably with the charges in operation in any town of similar size in the country.

The power house to-day is equipped with eight water-tube Babcock boilers with chain grate stokers which provide the steam for driving the four turbine driven alternators, capable of developing 23,250 kilowatts.

The following table shews the progress from 1908 to 31st March, 1927:

	STATISTICAL.	1908	1918	1927
1.	No. of units sold for Private Lighting	287,587	370,794	1,024,445
2.	No. of units sold for Public Lighting	37,739	19,689	134,912
3.	No. of units sold for Power and Heating	1,292,743	4,539,217	9,861,531
4.	No. of units sold for Traction (if any)	388,533	816,884	975,685
5.	Rateable value basis		152,436	744,086
6.	Bulk supplies		560,880	2,281,600
7.	Total number of units sold for all purposes	2,006,602	6,459,900	15,022,259
8.	No. of consumers	468	1,429	4,452
9.	Total connections in kilowatts	1,820	6,871	13,196
10.	Maximum demand in kilowatts	1,147	3,100	8,900
11.	Capacity of Station in kilowatts	1,888	6,325	13,000
12.	Load factor	22·7%	23·7%	24%
13.	Length of mains (in miles)	9.214	25.67	69.98

Financial

14.	Capital sanctioned	* £5,000 £67,960	*£5,000 £175,537	*£5,000 £500,249
15.	Capital expended	£68,858	£174,756	£502,021
16.	Capital repaid (loans)	£12,830	£56,395	£185,887
17.	Capital outstanding	£56,028	£108,109	£272,617
18.	Gross revenue	£11,878	£41,127	£93, 167
19.	Total working expenses, including management, rates, etc.	£7,338	£27,743	£57,887
20.	20. Loan charges; (a) Interest (b) Repayment of Principal	£1,729 £2,207	£5,037 £5,610	£12,541 £15,125
21.	Net profit	£604	£2,777	£4,668
22.	Depreciation or Reserve Funds in hand	£1,567	None	£4,790
23.	Total Works' costs, including management, rates, etc., per unit sold in pence	0.87	1.03	.9248
24.	Total capital charges per unit sold in pence	0.47	0.41	.4899
25.	(23· 24 together.)	1.34	1.44	1.4147
26.	Average price obtained	1.37	1.44	1.484

*For motors and apparatus under Accrington Corporation Act, 1905.

ELECTRICITY SHOWROOMS.

ELECTRICITY SHOWROOMS. Electricity Showrooms of a temporary nature were first established in the Post Office Arcade, Warner Street end, and later in Blackburn Road, at the junction of Eagle Street. During the war (in 1917), these premises were closed. No further steps were taken to secure permanent premises until 1925, when at a meeting of the Electricity Committee, on the 14th December, it was decided to secure the site at the junction of Burnley Road and Whalley Road, and erect new premises thereon after demolition of the old property. The work of demolition was put in hand and new showrooms erected by the Borough Surveyor, which were opened on the 10th March, 1927, by the Chairman of the Electricity Committee, Mr. Alderman Higham.

The cost of erection and equipment of the new premises, including demolition of the old property, was £4,325.

During the twelve months the Showrooms have been open, from the 1st April, 1927, to the 31st March, 1928, the value of electrical apparatus sold including cookers, boilers, irons, kettles, fires, etc., amounted to over £14,000.

TRAMWAYS.

THE Accrington Corporation laid the first tramway tracks in 1884-5-6, between Accrington and Church, Clayton-le-Moors, and Baxenden, and these were leased for a term of 21 years to the Accrington Corporation Steam Tramways Company.

On April 5th, 1886, the track was inspected by Major-General Hutchinson, R.E., Inspector for the Board of Trade. Two engines and a car were run over the length of track, and the Inspector authorized its use between Accrington and Church and Clayton for traffic, after a slight alteration at one point.

On Thursday, April 8th, 1886, the official opening of the Tramways took place. At 12-30p.m., cars proceeded from the Town Hall, containing Messrs. Cramp, Cosh, and Cubit of the Tramways Company, Alderman Hindle, Councillors Haythornthwaite, Broughton, A. Maden, and Woolley, and a number of prominent tradesmen. At Church, the party were joined by the Mayor of Accrington, Alderman Smith. From Church the cars travelled to Clayton and were met by Mr. J. Hacking and Mr. Towers, members of the Local Board, and Mr. Smith, Clerk. From Clayton-le-Moors the cars travelled back to the Town Hall, Accrington, where the Mayor addressed the assembled public.

From April 8th to 30th, 37,370 passengers were carried on three cars, the receipts amounting to £324 5s. 6d. During the month of May there were 39,768 passengers: an excellent commencement for the undertaking.

Saturday, June 12th, 1886, saw the Baxenden Section opened for traffic: the passenger figures and receipts at that period being: August, 81,049 (£621); September, 64,800 (£490); these figures rose in May, 1887, to 96,843 (£624).

On August 27th, 1887, the length of track from Baxenden to Haslingden was opened, and this section was further extended to Rawtenstall in November the same year.

The average number of passengers per week during the year 1888 was 38,000, and the weekly receipts totalled £270. The corresponding averages for 1905, were 43,000 and £310.

OLD STEAM TRAMS IN PEEL STREET.

In the Parliamentary Session of 1905, the Accrington Corporation promoted a Bill which gave them authority to reconstruct, equip, and work the tramways by electric power, and also to extend the tramways to Oswaldtwistle and Huncoat. The lease with the Accrington Steam Tramways Company expired on April 8th, 1907, and from April 12th to August 31st, 1907, the undertaking was operated jointly by the Corporation and the Tramways Company.

During the year 1907, the Corporation relayed the whole of the track and made extensions from Church to Oswaldtwistle and from Accrington to Huncoat.

Our illustration shews some of the old trams in Peel Street. Weird stories are current concerning the experiences of passengers, particularly in Manchester Road. Stories of assistance given by passengers in encouraging the engines to climb the hill. Too much credence cannot, perhaps, be given to them, but no one was sorry to see the last of the old steam trams, providing something took their place.

On Thursday, August 1st, 1907, the track between Accrington and Oswaldtwistle was inspected by Colonel Druitt, R.E., Inspector of the Board of Trade. He boarded a tramcar at Ellison Street, and was accompanied by the Mayor (Councillor T. E. Higham), Aldermen Bury and Rawson, the Town Clerk, Borough Surveyor, Tramways Manager, and Chief Constable, and on the way to Oswaldtwistle, the Chairman and Members of the Church and Oswaldtwistle District Council boarded the car. After the return to the Town Hall, Accrington, Colonel Druitt expressed himself as highly pleased with the work and at once gave permission for the use of the track for public service.

The formal opening of the Electric Tramways took place on Friday, August 2nd, 1907. At 10-0a.m., the Mayor (Councillor T. E. Higham), with the members of the Town Council and their wives, representatives of the Church and Oswaldtwistle Urban District Councils, travelled over the length of tramways, Accrington to Oswaldtwistle, in four gaily decorated tramcars, the first being driven by the Mayoress, Mrs. Higham, the second by Mrs. Rawson, the third by Mrs. A. S. Bury, and the fourth by Mrs. A. H. Aitken. On the return of the cars to the Town Hall, Accrington, the Mayor declared the Tramways open to the public.

Other Sections of the Tramways were opened as follows:
    Clayton-le-Moors Section on September 20th, 1907.
    Huncoat section on October 26th, 1907.
    Baxenden section on January 1st, 1908.

In September, 1908, the Haslingden Electric Tramways were opened, and from this date the car services have been operated by the Accrington Corporation.

Through running of tramcars between Accrington and Blackburn has been in operation since August, 1907, and between Accrington and Rawtenstall since April, 1910.

The following tables indicate the progress of the undertaking:

Year.	GROSS REVENUE. Accrington. £	Haslingden. £	Total. £	CAR MILEAGE. Accrington. £	Haslingden. £	Total. £
1907-8	11,761	-	11,761	238,109	-	238,109
1912-3	27,822	8,260	36,082	531,356	149,467	680,823
1917-8	36,713	10,558	47,271	529,488	147,277	676,765
1922-3	57,752	16,860	74,612	553,321	174,052	727,373
1927-8	54,416	14,992	69,408	600,709	186,343	787,052

PASSENGERS CARRIED.

Year.	Accrington.	Haslingden.	Total.
1907-8	2,116,772		2,116,772
1912-3	4,577,019	1,573,351	6,150,370
1917-8	5,831,742	1,813,428	7,645,170
1922-3	6,279,523	2,113,681	8,393,204
1927-8	8,900,079	2,449,558	11,399,637

Up to 31st March, 1928, the Corporation electric tramcars have covered 14,295,849 miles, the total number of passengers carried being 168,993,098, and it is gratifying to be able to record that not a single fatality has occurred nor has a passenger been seriously injured, There are 38 tramcars the maximum seating capacity of the larger type being 72 and the annual consumption of electricity is 1,275,000 units.

The capital cost of the undertaking is:

Permanent Way	£79,456
Electrical Equipment	19,343
Tramcars	40,333
Depot	14,167
Miscellaneous	10,008
Total	£163,307

The amount which has been repaid and is in hand for that purpose is £114,009, which leaves a liability of £49,298, and the depreciation and renewals fund is now £50,971. In the Accrington Corporation Parliamentary Bill, 1928, the Corporation are empowered to provide and work trolley vehicles and motor omnibuses. It is, therefore, anticipated that in the near future a service of omnibuses will be inaugurated.

AMBULANCE SERVICE.

The Corporation possesses two motor ambulances which are operated by the Tramways Department: a 35 h.p. Wolseley, presented to the Borough on October 13th, 1915, by Miss Haworth, of Hollins Hill, Accrington, in memory of her late brother William, and a 20 h.p. Austin, purchased in August, 1926. The ambulances serve the Borough of Accrington, and the Urban Districts of Church, Clayton-le-Moors, Huncoat, and Altham, and up to 31st March, 1928, have attended 4,766 calls and travelled 37,584 miles.

PUBLIC CLEANSING.

IN the minds of the uninitiated there is bound to be some confusion as to what exactly are the functions of a Cleansing Department. Primarily, these include Street Sweeping and all other operations employed in Street Cleansing, and the collection, removal, and disposal of household and trade refuse matters.

Many years ago, one of our most eminent men in the engineering world said: "The foundation of all Sanitary Science is scavenging, and if I were asked what is the most important feature of Sanitary Science I would repeat, scavenging. Your sewers, your drains, your water supply, are all secondary considerations if scavenging is neglected, and I say as a last word, mature your scavenging arrangements and make them perfect."

If these words were true very many years ago, how much more important must be their wise interpretation in these enlightened days? Quite irrespective of the many non-preventable insanitary areas in almost every town, there will always remain to be dealt with the natural filth products from the population and businesses connected with all towns. It is more especially on account of this latter factor, that within the past fifty years there has been brought to the front that great "preventable science" for the suppression of the causes of disease, "Cleansing" as applied through the machinery of a Cleansing Department under the control of a Cleansing Superintendent. Fifty years ago this Department was created in some of our larger cities much as a luxury, but to-day, the smallest town looks upon it as an absolute necessity.

STREET CLEANSING. The total mileage of streets and roadways, including the new Housing Estates of the Borough, is 56.65, in addition to some 3,765 square yards of market grounds.

In 1914, the mileage was 44, and the number of men engaged in carrying out the work of Street Cleansing was 26, including a foreman. Although more than 12 miles have been added to the area to be scavenged by this Department since 1914, the number of hands remains the same. This is partly accounted for by the tremendous increase in the use of motor transport which has taken the place largely of the horse, less sweepings being produced. The use of a mechanical Sweeper and Collector has also contributed to the efficiency of these operations, besides accelerating the work, without interfering with modern traffic conditions on busy main roads.

Our main shopping thoroughfares are swept daily, five miles of main roadways are swept three times weekly, whilst the remainder are attended to not less than once weekly, principally by hand sweeping. Street sweepings are mixed with manure from the Public Abattoirs, certain market refuse, and with fine dust screened from household refuse, the resultant compound producing a manure which commands a ready sale amongst farmers and others within a radius of about five miles of the Salvage and Destructor Works. The net expenditure on Street Cleansing for the financial year 1926-27, was £3,655, being equal to a rate of 3.6d. in the pound.

COLLECTION AND DISPOSAL OF HOUSE AND TRADE REFUSE.

(1) COLLECTION: Before the introduction of the petrol motor for refuse collection in 1920, the Borough was for this purpose divided into seven districts, with a horse, cart, driver, and ashpit-man to each district. The total hands numbered 14, the ashpit-men being responsible for their own districts. The annual yield of house and shop refuse was about 10,000 tons. At the present time the Borough is divided into three districts with a two-ton petrol motor to each, and in addition a horse and four-wheeled cart are employed on the shorter hauls within a radius of about half a mile from the Disposal Works. As occasion demands, an extra horse and cart is employed to relieve congestion in anyone district. The annual yield of refuse is now from 12,000 to 13,000 tons. The total hands employed on refuse collection for the most part of the year is still 14, which, as indicated, is increased to 16 as occasion demands.

The Health Committee now possesses most of the transport required for its own work, and in addition to the mechanical Road Sweeper-Collector mentioned, it is responsible for the running, repair, and management of five petrol vehicles, which are housed at the Hyndburn Road Depot. The refuse yield per capita in Accrington is considered to be too high, and there are experts in cleansing matters who have proved that the wholesale abolition of ash pits and the substitution therefor of galvanized iron dust bins with covers, is the surest means of reducing refuse yield at its source. Our yield is about 16 to 17 cwts. per 1,000 of the population per day, whereas in one large city, by the introduction of bins, the yield has fallen under 10 cwts. per 1,000 of the population.

(2) DISPOSAL: Prior to the year 1900, house and shop refuse was disposed of by depositing it on various tips in the Borough, certain organic matter being burned at Ward's works at Milnshaw. In 1900, a Destructor was installed. The plant which was built by the Horsfall Destructor Company at a cost of £8,000, consisted of a six-cell Destructor with two Lancashire Boilers, the whole being designed for steam raising purposes in conjunction with the Electricity undertaking. The Health Committee controlled the Destructor, and the Electricity Committee, who utilised the steam so produced, controlled the boilers. The Health Committee received 11d. per ton for all refuse destroyed, which was calculated on the basis of coal costs with coal at that time at about 12/- per ton. As time went on Mortar Mills were installed, which went far to solve the problem of clinker disposal. Any scheme which prevents the re-carting of refuse from the Destructor in the form of clinker, and on the other hand turns the clinker to valuable account, is sound economics. This was eventually achieved, large quantities of screened clinker, in the form of concrete being used by the Surveyor's Department, in place of rubble pitching and broken stone for the under-bedding of roads. As time went on the Electricity Station adjoining the Destructor Works, grew in dimensions, and for many years it was evident that the old Destructor, which had been in operation since 1900, would have to be replaced. Plans and drawings for extensions were considered by the Health Committee in 1914, but war conditions put a stop temporarily to the scheme. Part of the scheme, however, was carried out during 1916-17, the works consisting of a new chimney, dust-catcher, water-tube boiler and flues, etc., at a cost of £7,000. The old Destructor furnaces were not at that time altered, but were connected to the new chimney, this arrangement giving the

Electricity Department better facilities for working and extending their plant.

In 1922, tenders were invited for a new Destructor and Mechanical Salvage Plant, the scheme involving alterations to the existing Destructor buildings, Messrs. Heenan and Froude Ltd., Engineers, of Worcester, were the successful tenderers the same firm, by the way, who were responsible for the erection of the Blackpool Tower. The tender was accepted subject to the approval of the Ministry of Health, and at the subsequent enquiry held by J. C. Dawes, Esq., O.B.E., loan sanction was obtained, the work being put in hand in 1924. The new works were opened in March, 1925.

The total cost of the complete scheme was about £30,000. The plant, as newly opened, comprised a six-cell top-feed continuous-grate incinerator; two Babcock and Wilcox's watertube boilers, each with a heating surface of 1,966 square feet, fitted with superheaters; chimney and dust catcher; Royce electric hoist and Barnard grab for transporting refuse to the screen; revolving screen for extracting dust from refuse; conveyor belt with magnetic separator for dealing with the metallic portion of the refuse; belt and gear for automatically distributing the burnable portion of the refuse over the Destructor furnace openings; clinker crushing, screening and grading machinery; plant for the manufacture of tarred clinker for roadways; four mortar mills; hydraulic press for bundling scrap tins, etc.; hand-baling presses for waste paper, and a complete unit for the manufacture of feeding meal from fish offal. Steam raised by the Destructor is still passed by pipeline to the Electricity Generating Station adjoining the works. The plant described has now been working as a whole for over three years, and is giving satisfaction. When it is considered that there is over thirty thousand pounds worth of plant, which is being operated under really bad conditions, inasmuch as the material handled is gritty and putrefactive, and entails constant care and attendant renewals, the task of controlling the Department as a whole, comprising as it does, Medical Services, Sanitary Inspection, and Public Cleansing and Salvage, is of very considerable import. The reduction in the cost of refuse collection and disposal per annum, together with the number of houses served in the Borough, may best be illustrated by comparing the figures for 1921 and 1927:

Year.	Refuse Collection and Disposal. £	No. of Houses Served.
1921	13,857	11,238
1927	8,851	11,851

It may also be of interest to learn to what extent various forms of salvage and the utilization of residuals are carried out by the Department, as indicated by the figures for the year ended 31st December, 1927. Fish Meal, £1,220 16s. 3d.; Baled Scrap Tins, £288 11s. 8d.; Baled Waste Paper, £232 2s. 1d.; Tar Macadam, £107 7s. 10d.; Baled Bagging, Carpets, and Rugs, £49 16s. 8d.; Street Sweepings, £46 5s. 10d.; Light Scrap Iron, £28 4s. 9d.; Rags, £14 2S. 5d.; Cast Scrap Iron, £7 15s. 6d.; Scrap Lead, £6 15s. 0d.; Glass, £5 2s. 5d.; Fat, £3 18s. 5d.; String, £2 19s. 0d.; Bones, £2 12s. 0d.; Scrap Brass, £1 18s. 1d.; Hair, 11/6; Mortar, £2,038 4s. 1d.; Clinker, £64 10s. 0d.; Calorific Power-contribution from Electricity Department for refuse burnt, £800 0s. 0d. Total amount realized, £4,921 13s. 6d.

CEMETERY.

ST. JAMES'S Churchyard was the only burial ground for many years. It was added to from time to time, the first addition, according to the Rev. J. T. Lawrence, was in 1814. This was, in all likelihood, the result of the following resolution of the vestry "Whereas, on Sunday, the 9th day of October, 1808, public notice was given in time of divine service, in the Chapel of Accrington, for the inhabitants of Old and New Accrington, to meet in vestry on Thursday, the 20th of the said month, to take into consideration the necessity of making an addition to the burial ground of the Chapel of Accrington aforesaid. We, whose names are underwritten, being the majority of the said vestry and having duly considered the very urgent necessity of making addition to the said burial ground, do hereby empower and authorize the Chapel Wardens for the time being, with all possible expedition to make additions to the burial ground, aforesaid, in such proportion, and at such. . . . quarters as they may think best, as witness our hands, this 20th day of October, 1808.

   Geo. Park, Off's. Minister.
   Robert Peel.
   Geo. Pickup.
   John Rothwell."

The average annual mortality in Accrington (New and Old) for the ten years ending 1847, was 201, "which, although small when compared with that of most of the other towns in the County of Lancaster, cannot be considered to indicate a satisfactory state of health" (Babbage).

MACHPELAH.

In all there were six burial grounds in Accrington in 1850. St. James's Churchyard was still the main one, for in 1846, out of the 263 persons registered as dying in the town that year, 137 were interred there. Christ Churchyard, which was of recent adoption and was then "quite on the outskirts of the town." The New Jerusalem Burial Ground in Abbey Street, facing the chapel, where the interments averaged about fifteen annually. The Independent Burial Ground in Oak Street commenced in 1842, but was little used, only 20 burials being recorded to 1850. A portion of the burial ground was above the level of the floor used as a schoolroom. The Wesleyan Burial Ground in Union Street, which was opened in 1807 and to 1850 had totalled 780 interments; and, finally, the Baptists' Burial Ground "in Allom-lane" known as Machpelah. Mr. Babbage recommended that no further interments should be allowed in the old part of St. James's Churchyard, nor in the New Jerusalem or the Wesleyan Grounds, and that so long as the lower part of the Independent Chapel was used as a school, interments should be prohibited there. A strong recommendation in favour of a general cemetery was made.

The first move in this direction occurred when the Local Board made an order in 1858, for closing the burial grounds.

In the month of October, 1864, a plot of land, some twenty acres in extent, was laid out as a cemetery. The first interment took place on the l0th of that month, when the remains of Mr. William Barnes, one of the chief advocates of providing a cemetery, were laid to rest. Provision was made for 17,684 grave spaces. The cost of laying out, making the roads and paths, draining the land, and building three churches, the Registrar's house, and other offices, was £10,164. In recent years considerable sums have been spent in repairs to the churches, and about £1,500 in repairing and renewing the paths and roads.

In 1926, the Corporation purchased some twenty-six acres of land for necessary extensions, the widening of Burnley Road, and the formation of new streets, such as Livingstone Road and Church Street, Huncoat. Allowing for these street improvements a net twenty-four and a half acres of land remain for the purposes of the cemetery, estimated to allow for 20,000 grave spaces. The cost of the land was £2,950, and the estimated cost of laying out, main drainage, construction of roads, paths, erection of boundary walls, and rebuilding Registrar's house and other offices, is £24.400.

The number of interments varies little, for if you take the last year in a decade beginning with 1874 (the first full ten years), they are as follows: 1864-1874, 520; 1874-1884, 547; 1884-1894, 560; 1894-1904, 625; 1904-1914, 514; 1914-1924, 511. These figures show a slight decline in recent years, and a considerable one for the last two periods in comparison with the first, having regard to the differences in the total population. No doubt the establishment of the Church and Clayton-le-Moors Joint Cemetery has had some effect, but it also shows an increase in the length of individual lives; pointing to improved sanitation and the health of the people. The total number of interments from the beginning up to December 31st, 1927, is 41,995 nearly the equivalent of the present population.

MARKETS.

ACCRINGTON has, for centuries, been looked upon as the marketing centre for the district. The Court Roll of November 1547, bears witness to the presence of a corn market in the sixteenth century. One Oliver Birtwistle complained against six other persons that they had stopped his way to and from "the Kynges Cowrte of Accryington, the Kynges mylne, the Churche, the Kynges Fold, and the Kinges markett." Two of the six recanted, but the other four persisting, the case was referred to be "tryed by xxiiij Customers of the venew of the Olde Tenur with Blackeburneshir." Oliver gained all his points save the right of way to the Markett. The Corn Market continued until the early nineteenth century at the Lower Fold. Later records shew the use of Warner Street and Abbey Street for market purposes until the present Market House was established in 1869 (See "Local Board of Health Days"). The Tuesday Market was established on April 16th, 1872. A fire occurred in the Hall on June 13th, 1880, which did damage to the extent of £3,000.

The Capital Expenditure on the Market has been £29,352. Connected therewith further land and property has been purchased in Peel Street and Pleck Road for extensions, at a cost of £9,712; a total of £39,064, and with the Dutton Street Lavatories, which are worked in connection with the Markets (£1,290), a total outlay of £40,354. Of this figure the debt remaining is as follows: On Market House, £5,195; On Peel Street and Pleck Road property, £8,992; on

Dutton Street Lavatories, £604; making the loans owing, £14,791. In 1878-79, the Market tolls were leased, and after deducting therefrom the expenses, there was a profit of £97. For 1927-28, the profits were almost £2,000.

WEIGHTS AND MEASURES.

"AT a Vestry meeting, held on the 28th February, 1828, it was agreed that any deficiency wanting to purchase weights and measures for the use of the townships of Old and New Accrington be defrayed by the said townships according to their respective proportions. The Innkeepers, Shopkeepers, etc., etc., have subscribed upwards of £50 towards the purchase of the said weights and measures. It is further ordered that Mr. Charles be requested to write to London for the weights and measures, and that he procure them with all possible expedition." It will be observed that this was the Mr. Charles appointed Secretary to the Lighting Inspectors in 1841.

"Also, at a meeting held May 22nd, 1828, it was resolved that Joseph Booth is a fit and proper person to be appointed to examine the weights and measures, etc., in these townships, and that he be nominated for the approval of the magistrates for that purpose, and that he be indemnified any expenses incurred by him in procuring such appointment." The sequel to this appointment is recorded under the section "The Police." From this good beginning the town has not retracted and this section is now a recognized part of municipal activity.

There is no debt on this Department, the equipment having been bought out of revenue. The income for 1928-29, is estimated at £100 from fees for stamping, adjusting, etc., £240 from the Lancashire County Council, proportion of County Rate refunded, giving receipts of £340. The expenditure is estimated at £260; leaving the net receipts £80.

THE TOWN HALL.

THE Town Hall, first known as the Peel Institution, originally built as a memorial to Sir Robert Peel at a cost of £11,000, was opened on December 24th, 1858. It had been necessary to form a Company to carry the project through, and in 1859, the Institution was let to the Mechanics' Institution. The Peel Institution was purchased by the Local Board in April, 1865, for £4,000, the Mechanics' Institution retained their tenancy until October, 1878. Its lower portions served as municipal offices entirely until 1909, when the Finance and the Education Departments were transferred to Gothic House, which had been purchased with this object in view: the cost being £2,100. With the growth of municipal activity, there is pressing need for further accommodation to be provided.

FIRE BRIGADE AND LIGHTING.

THE Fire Brigade and Street Lighting Departments are combined. In addition to the Borough, the Fire Brigade serves the districts of Church, Clayton-le-Moors, Altham, and Huncoat, the Councils of these authorities pay to the Corporation their proportionate share of the costs of the Brigade.

The equipment consists of: One Merryweather Motor Fire Engine fitted up with Pump of 500 gallons per minute capacity, and also carrying 60ft. Fire Escape. One Merryweather Motor Fire Engine fitted with pump of 350 gallons per minute capacity, with extension ladders of 35ft. One Lancia tender carrying extension ladders. One Ford chassis fitted up with Dennis Turbine Pump of 150 gallons per minute capacity. The net cost of the Brigade is £1,540, equal to a rate of 1½d. in the £.

The Street Lighting is done by both Gas and Electricity, there being 900 Gas Lamps and 570 Electric Lamps. The cost of this Department is £4,870, equal to a rate of 4¾d. in the £.

(Particulars of the early. history of these departments will be found in the chapter "The Old Lighting and Watching Days."-Ed.)

PARKS.

ACCRINGTON is well provided with public parks. The earliest attempt by the town to secure ground for this purpose was in 1879 (October 17th), when the Corporation purchased what was known as Victoria Gardens, now Milnshaw Park. It was opened by the Mayor (Alderman Lightfoot), on July 17th, 1880. £500 was spent in securing the former owner's interest, and £2,000 upon laying the grounds out. It was only small, being under six acres in extent, and doubt was expressed in the press as to the possibility of growing anything in it. It was placed under the control of the Watch and Cemetery Committee, and has fully justified its existence as a breathing-space in a part of the town where some such amenity is needed. In addition to the playground it has two bowling-greens and nine tennis courts.

The idea of acquiring Oak Hill grounds and mansion was first brought to the notice of the Town Council in 1890, and after considerable negotiation it was secured for the public as noted under the paragraph relating to the Museum. It was opened by Mr. Reginald G. Hargreaves on Whit-Monday, May 22nd, 1893. Huge crowds attended the opening ceremony which was made an occasion of public rejoicing. This was not the only official incident of that Whit-Monday, for during the afternoon the Mayor presented the two pieces of artillery still to be seen, and Councillor Joseph Duxbury, the bandstand. The park is a natural one of considerable beauty, standing on rising ground midway between the old and the new roads to Manchester. Originally consisting of 13½ acres, it has been extended recently (1920), and now covers an area of 15½ acres. It affords opportunities for bowls and tennis, containing two bowling-greens and five hard courts. The aviary, which has been enriched by many gifts, is a feature of its interest to visitors. In the higher portion there has been erected Accrington's memorial to those who fell in the great world war, which was unveiled by H. H. Bolton, Esq., on the 1st July, 1922.

MILNSHAW PARK.

OAK HILL PARK.

OAK HILL PARK.

OPENING OF OAK HILL PARK.

Peel Park, familiarly known as the Coppice, consists of some 92½ acres on an eminence on the easterly side of the town. 57½ acres were purchased, and 35 given by the owner, Mr. William Peel, of Knowlmere. The negotiations had continued for some years but were successfully concluded, and the Park opened by Mr. Peel, on Wednesday, September 29th, 1909. Hillock Farm, now part of Peel Park, was at one time the residence of the Riley family, from whom Edward Croston purchased it in the seventeenth century. This Edward Croston, in the Civil War Tax return, was assessed at £25, the highest amount of any in Old Accrington. He married a niece of Humphrey Chetham of Manchester fame. The Hillock is identified as the Fernihalgh Vaccary.

In September, 1913, the Council accepted, with an expression of their appreciation, the gift of some 46 acres of land in Spring Hill district, by Mr. Tom Bullough, in memory of his grandfather, to be known as the "James Bullough" Park. Parts have been used for allotment purposes, but its use for recreational purposes has been developed of late until it now has three bowling-greens and three tennis courts, with facilities for the playing of other games. Messrs.

Howard and Bullough Ltd., presented the tennis courts and pavilion in 1926.

HILLOCK FARM.

BULLOUGH PARK AND PRIESTLEY CLOUGH.

Still another open space was added to the town's open-air amenities when, in November, 1920, the Council received an intimation that by the will of the late Miss Anne Haworth, the house and land known as "Hollins Hill," were to be given to the town, together with an endowment of £28,000, for the purposes of a Park and Art Gallery. The gift was gratefully accepted, and the Park and Gallery opened on September 21st, 1921. The gift also included a number of pictures, furniture and effects, and these, together with the art objects previously collected are on exhibition at Haworth Art Gallery.

The collection numbers some one hundred and fifty pictures. It would be impossible to mention the very generous donations which have made up the collection now to be seen at the Gallery. One of the foremost gifts in addition to that already named, was the bequest of the late Mrs. Geo. Nuttall.

The town is now seeking to increase the number of open spaces which may be used as playing fields, and this outline of Accrington's spacious parks and grounds would be incomplete without reference to the Mayor and Mayoress's gift this Jubilee year, of land at Pennyhouse some 13 acres in extent which is to be developed. Additional land, too, has been secured to the west of Hollins Lane, known as Hollins Farm Estate, part of which is to be used for playing-field purposes, probably some 30 acres.

HAWORTH ART GALLERY.

THE MUSEUM.

THIS building presents the finest example of old Georgian style of architecture in Accrington. A plan dated 1807, gives the owner of Oak Hill house as Daniel Henry Woodward, of Boswell, Gloucestershire. He assumed the name of Lee-Warner on inheriting Walsingham Abbey, Norfolk, and died in 1835. Thomas Hargreaves, born in Wheatley Lane, Pendle Forest, in 1771, built Oak Hill Mansion in 1793, on the old site and foundations of the original building. In 1802, this Thomas Hargreaves removed to Oakenshaw House, Clayton-le-Moors, which he built. He returned to Oak Hill in 1812, demolished the whole structure, and built the present mansion about 1815, the land being leased to him for the term of 999 years. Later, Jonathan Hargreaves, son of Thomas, enlarged the building by the addition of a new wing, the present Mineral and Historical room. The house was subsequently occupied by other Accrington families, but for some years it remained vacant, and was eventually purchased by the Corporation. The cost of the mansion and grounds was £12,048, towards which Mr. Reginald G. Hargreaves generously contributed £1,000. Sanction to borrow the purchase money was obtained in July, 1892. The purchase was not effected without considerable discussion, which led eventually to the matter being referred to the electors, whose votes resulted in a majority of 1,286 in favour of the purchase. The house was opened as a Museum in 1900, Mr. Wigglesworth being appointed Curator. The collection is housed in eight rooms, with a floor space of over 4,000 square feet. Its inception is due principally to the generosity of the granddaughter of Thomas Hargreaves, the late Mrs. Robertson-Aikman, who presented the splendid collections of her cousin, the late Colonel Rimington, an ardent collector, consisting principally of mineral, botanical, and entomological specimens, in addition to many gifts of her own ceramics, corals, shells, etc. The Naturalists' Society also handed over their collection.

The material was re-arranged and classified by Dr. B. W. Gerland and his son, Dr. Conrad Gerland. In 1918, the "Accrington and District Historical Association" was formed, pioneered by "Accrington Friend and Well-Wisher" whose generosity has resulted in a magnificent collection of photographs of Accrington's past worthies, historical sites, and local events, contained in ebonized stands, also mahogany bookcases containing a reference library of Lancashire works. A recent acquisition is the late Mr. Richard Broughton's collection of books, deeds, documents, etc., numbering over 700 items.

THE WAR MEMORIAL.

The following are the chief exhibits in the Museum. The Entrance Hall contains pictures of travel-scenes from Naples, Milan, etc., and examples of animal heads and horns. Room one houses the botanical and zoological exhibits, the former comprising some 15,000 specimens of economic and medicinal plants, seaweeds, ferns, lichens, etc. The British birds' eggs are arranged in clutches, some 300 species being represented. The mineral section is contained in Room two, and is arranged in part according to Dana's System of Mineralogy; it includes some 10,000 specimens. In this room will also be found some 150 bronze medals. The mineral specimens are continued in Room three, which also houses the palaeontological exhibits arranged in sequence and periods; the carboniferous specimens number over 2,000. This room also contains over 500 specimens of British and foreign birds, representing some 200 species. Room four, entitled the Rimington Room, has in it the magnificent collection of butterflies, moths, and beetles of the late Colonel Rimington. This collection has many exquisite examples from all parts of the world, totalling some 50,000. One of the largest examples is an Atlas moth of India, with a wing spread of 10¼ inches. The British items alone number over 20,000, and include rare and extinct specimens.

Ascending to the first floor, in Room five may be found many excellent examples of the potter's art, including a set of old English and Dutch Lustre Ware. This room also contains the preserved specimens of fresh-water fish, sponges, sea urchins, etc., and some 6,000 shells out of a total of some 25,000.

In Room six will be found, among other things, some excellent reproductions of Italian art, an old seventeenth century spinning-wheel, and the Corbel stones from the old Black Abbey.

Further examples of shells are to be found in Room seven, some delicate examples of corals, cases containing birds and animals, and ethnological specimens. This room also contains the Reference Library of the Accrington and District Historical Association, some 360 volumes.

Room eight is known as the Historical Room, where, in addition to a display of some 3,000 coins, medals, and tokens, including the William Ashworth gift, examples of the goldsmith's art will be found. The most important exhibit in this room is that of the collection of photographs of old Accrington, already referred to.

During the twenty-eight years of its existence, the Museum has been enriched by many gifts, and is now well equipped and worthy to take its place as one of our educational institutions. The Museum will cost close upon £500 for the year 1928-29.

THE MUSEUM.

THE PUBLIC BATHS.

THE Public Baths were opened in June, 1879, by the then Mayor (Mr. John E. Lightfoot). They were public in the sense that they were open to all comers at a moderate charge, but were not owned by the town. They owe their inception to the enthusiasm of Mr. Eli Higham (a member of the Council), who erected them at his own cost. Hope was expressed, even at the opening ceremony, that the town would eventually take them over. The plunge bath was 43 feet by 17, and was made of iron, the water being conveyed from Mr. Higham's supply at Woodnook. In the front portion there was a refreshment room where sweets, tea, coffee, etc., could be purchased from the Baths Keepers, Mr. and Mrs. Oldham. The opening ceremony was made a public affair, music being supplied by the "Accrington Serenade Band." The suggestion of town ownership did not mature until 1893, when the Baths were purchased by the Corporation for £1,400. They served the needs of the community more or less satisfactorily for eighteen years, during the greater part of which period correspondents urged, in the press, the need for better bathing accommodation. A Public Baths does not appear to offer the best opportunities for a fire, but it must be remembered the old building was largely composed of wood. A fire, however, did occur in November, 1903, and damage to the extent of £600 to £700 was done. This increased the outcry for new baths, and the present building was erected on the plans and designs prepared by the Borough Surveyor (Mr. W. J. Newton), at a cost of £10,132-£1,050 for the site, £9,082 for the building and opened by the Mayor (Alderman A. S. Bury), on April l0th, 1911. The cry is still for more, and at the moment there is talk of an additional swimming bath vacant land adjoining the baths being sufficient for one to be erected.

The present building contains 16 Private Baths and a Swimming Pond 75 feet by 30, with a depth varying from three feet six inches to six feet nine inches. 41 cubicles are provided. The necessary machinery for washing and drying towels and for the supply of hot water has also been provided. A recent addition to the apparatus is the installation of a Bell's filtration plant, at a cost of £3,568, by means of which the water is constantly filtered, aerated, and heated.

Since the Committee engaged an instructor and an instructress in swimming, there has been a notable increase in the number of attendances, particularly of school children who average an attendance of one thousand per week. The Schools' Swimming Association is a strong and active institution, and has done much to foster interest in swimming and develop the keenness displayed by the children at their Annual Gala. The competition for the Cup and Shields between the various teams representing the schools is exceedingly keen. Instruction in Life Saving is not neglected, the competition for the Gordon Snell Shield and the Gold Medal arouses great interest. Last year, 240 certificates were awarded to school children for proficiency in swimming. There has also been a noticeable increase in the number of Lady Swimmers, the average daily attendance on the day reserved for ladies is 614. The cost of the Baths for 1928-29 is estimated at £1,310.

THE PUBLIC BATHS (INTERIOR).

The Accrington Borough Swimming Club is a progressive body and has its headquarters at the Baths. They have exclusive use of the Baths on two evenings per week, and are members of the North Lancashire Polo and Squadron League. For the year ended 31st March, 1928, the number of persons using the Private Baths was 16,373; and the Plunge Baths, 57,495 (14,215 adults, 43,280 children). 410 contracts were issued, the attendances with these numbering 19,941.

ABATTOIRS.

MR. BABBAGE, in his report of 1850, makes very strong comment upon the method of slaughtering cattle, and the disposal of the refuse. The Local Board realized the importance of making proper provision for slaughter houses towards the latter end of their term when they purchased land with the object of erecting a suitable building, but it was not until the 1st May, 1891, that the Abattoirs were opened. They were erected at a cost of £11,150. Of this amount, £7,011 has been repaid, leaving the loan debt at 31st March, 1928, £4,139. The estimated working expenses for 1928-29, are £690, plus debt charges, £580; a total of £1,270. The receipts from tolls are expected to be £620, leaving the net cost for the year at £650.

STABLES.

THE Stables were opened on August 22nd, 1890, and were built at a cost of £4,579, of which there is owing only £1,797. In conjunction with the Stables there is run a Smithy and a Wheelwrights' Department, which carries out work for the various departments of the Corporation.

The three departments combined are self-supporting, not having made calls upon the rates for many years. A stock of about 20 horses is maintained for the services of the Corporation.

GENERAL FINANCE.

At the time the Charter of Incorporation was applied for, the Rateable value of the town was £90,315.

	In	1888 it was	£120,872
		1898 it was	£154,570
		1908 it was	£185,711
		1918 it was	£207,700
		and in 1928 it is	£275,388

The Rates of the Borough for the corresponding years have been as follows:

	Boro' Rate.	Education.	General District.	Total for Corporation.	Poor and County Rate.	Total.
	s. d.	s. d.	s. d.	s. d.	s. d.	s. d.
1878	0 8	-	2 4	3 0	1 4	4 4
1888	0 11½	-	2 2	3 1½	1 0½	4 2
1898	1 0	-	3 4	4 4	1 2	5 6
1908	1 0¼	1 2	3 6	5 8¼	1 3¾	7 0
1918	1 3¾	1 4¾	3 8	6 4½	2 8½	9 1
1928	1 8	2 1¾	4 0	7 9¾	4 2¼	12 0

The highest rate levied was in the year 1921-22, the peak year so far as prices were concerned, and amounted to 15/3 in the £. In the following year there was a decrease of 1/9 to 13/6. In 1923-24, there was a further drop of 2/- to 11/6, and for the two succeeding years, 1924-25 and 1925-26, a drop of 8d. to 10/10. From that time slight increases of 2d. in 1926-27, 6d. in 1927-28, and 6d. in this year have taken place, making the present rate 12/- in the £.

In 1878-79 a penny rate realized a sum of £360.

In 1928-29 a penny rate is estimated to produce £1,053.

The amounts produced by the Rates in 1878-79 compared with what is estimated for 1928-29, are as follows:

	1878-79	1928-29
District Rate	£8,800	£49,820
Borough Rate	£2,900	£48,300
Poor and County Rate	£5,800	£52,790
	£17,500	£150,910

The following figures of the Poor Rates in earlier days are of interest by way of comparison:

Price per £.

May 5th,	1836	Old Accrington	5/-
May 5th,	1836	New Accrington	1/9
July 13th,	1837	Old Accrington	3/-
July 13th,	1837	New Accrington	2/-
September 22nd,	1838	Old and New Accrington	2/-
September 9th,	1839	Old and New Accrington	2/-
May 25th,	1840	Old and New Accrington	3/-

The only assets of the Borough on its formation were:

	£.
Town Hall and Offices	5,050
Markets	28,300
Cemetery	10,170
Main Sewers	9,653
Street Lamps	2,000
A total of	£53,173

The Capital expenditure taken over from the old Local Board was £55,173, of which £10,788 had been repaid, leaving loan indebtedness of £44,385. The Capital expenditure has been increased until in 1927-28, it amounted to £1,377,000, of which £600,000 has been repaid, leaving loan indebtedness of £777,000. Against this figure, the Corporation are the owners of assets to a value of £1,633,000, so that there is a surplus of assets over liabilities of £856,000.

INSURANCE. The Corporation covers its own risks under the Workmen's Compensation Acts, having formed a fund for that purpose, to which each Department contributes annually according to the proportion of wages paid. The Fund has been in existence since 1912-13, and had a credit balance at 31st March, 1928, of £3,050. A Fire Insurance Fund was also established under the Corporation Act of 1905, and, having had no claims thereon, has accumulated a balance of £7,610.

CHARITIES. A Fund, known as the Duxbury Charity Account, was founded from a Bequest by the late Joseph Duxbury, at one time a Councillor of the Borough. The Bequest was of the value of £3,000, which is invested with the Corporation, and the income therefrom, amounting to £150 per annum, is distributed to "Aged and necessitous poor" of the Borough.

SUPERANNUATION FUND. The Corporation have adopted, under the Local Government and other Officers' Superannuation Act, 1922, a scheme of Superannuation for both Officials and Workmen. The "Appointed Day" for the commencement of the scheme was 1st October, 1925.

To 31st March, 1928, six officials and ten Workmen had retired, and are receiving the amount of Superannuation due to them.

The fund is a contributory one on the basis of 5% from the Corporation, and 5% from the Employees, together with an equalized annual contribution by the Corporation to provide for the non-contributory service of the employees prior to the "Appointed Day." At the 31st March, 1928, the Fund had accumulated a sum of £11,600.

ACCRINGTON AND DISTRICT GAS AND WATER SUPPLY.

ACCRINGTON Gas and Water supply may be said to date back to the year 1840, when several local gentlemen formed themselves into a Committee to consider the formation of a Company for the supplying of the townships of Old and New Accrington with Gas and Water.

The Company was first incorporated by an Act of Parliament passed in 1841, 4 Vic. cap. 27, intituled "An Act to light with Gas and supply with Water the townships of Old and New Accrington and Church in the County Palatine of Lancaster." The preamble of this Act recites that "The townships of Old and New Accrington and Church are large and populous places and it is expedient that the houses, shops, factories, streets, etc., therein be lighted with Gas and that the townships of Old and New Accrington are not, at present well supplied with Water and the inhabitants thereof are thereby subjected to much inconvenience and liable to great danger in cases of accident or fire, which inconvenience and danger might be prevented if a constant supply of water were obtained and conveyed to the said townships." The names of the parties associated together to promote the Act were, the Rev. John Hopwood, Messrs. Hargreaves, Stansfield, Steiner, Dewhurst, Hepple, Lang, Christie, Grimshaw, Briggs, Cunliffe, Radcliffe, Nutter, Hindle, and many other old Accrington family names; ninety-three in all.

The first water supply came from Hillock Bank Spring. The townships at that time contained about 800 houses, and it was estimated that each house would require eight gallons per day.

The first reservoir, situated in Burnley Road, Huncoat, was constructed in 1841; it covered half a Lancashire acre and was estimated to contain two and a half million gallons sufficient to give six gallons per day to each house for one and a half years. The anticipated revenue was £400 per annum, being five per cent. on £8,000, the total rental of the town. The second reservoir at Burnley Road, Huncoat, was constructed about 1849.

During these years, 1841 to 1849, the Gas Works, situated in Hyndburn Road, was constructed and added to several times, the gas output increasing, but no record is available as to the actual figures. The coal was brought by canal to Alleytroyd's Wharf, Church, and unloaded there for the Accrington works.

The problem of collecting some of the Water Accounts appears to have given trouble as far back as 1851, it being recorded that in October of that year, the Collector be empowered to allow Mr. J. Cronshaw, Auctioneer, two pence in the shilling on all the "desperate" water accounts he may collect for the Company.

The year 1853, saw a considerable advance in the activities of the Company, as an application was made to Parliament for further powers to supply Gas and Water and to include the townships of Hapton, Huncoat, Altham, Clayton-le-Moors, Church, Oswaldtwistle, Henheads, and Lower Booths.

The following year the Local Board of Health approached the Company on the question of purchasing the Undertaking, but it was turned down by the Shareholders. The year 1855, saw the work commenced on the construction of the first reservoir at Mitchell's House, this being completed in 1860.

In 1859, the inhabitants of Clayton-le-Moors petitioned the Company for a supply of water to that township.

The Gas Works, originally constructed for the Oakenshaw Printworks, was purchased by the Company in 1862, and the Gas Works at Great Harwood (which was incorporated in 1856), was taken over by the Company in 1863.

The year 1864, saw the land secured for the present Dean Reservoir, and a service reservoir constructed at Cliffe, Great Harwood, on the site of the present Filtering Station. A water supply for Rishton was first discussed during the year 1866, and the following year the Accrington Local Board again approached the Company with a view to taking over the Undertaking. The Company also turned down this and a further like proposal in 1874.

The construction of Dean Reservoir took place about 1872, and the second reservoir at Mitchell's, about 1876.

The year 1885, records the provision of a water supply for Huncoat, while the following year considerable trouble was experienced with the Mitchell's Reservoirs, due to coal mining operations underneath them.

Further attempts made by the Local Authorities to purchase the Company's Undertakings, took place during 1890 and 1891, and these ultimately terminated in the formation of the present Board during 1894. The gas output at this time was 290 million cubic feet per annum, and the number of consumers 13,913, the revenue income being £46,192. The water supplied approximated 1,473,000 gallons per day, equal to 21 gallons per head of population. The Revenue income being £17,619.

A few notes on the progress of the undertaking under the Board's regime may be of interest.

WATER. Immediately after the formation of the Board, the question of the water supply appears to have received special attention. New filters, pumps, and a covered reservoir were constructed at Cliffe, Great Harwood, during 1899, and filtering tanks installed at Mitchell's during 1903.

The year 1906, saw powers obtained for sinking the Bore-hole at Altham, and this work was completed and a pump installed during 1908. This supply has yielded an average of about 150 million gallons per annum since its inception.

A second Bore-hole is now in process of sinking into the lower water-bearing stratum, about 350 feet below ground level, which it is expected will yield an abundant supply of pure water with but a moderate degree of hardness.

A scheme is also being prepared for storing this water in a covered reservoir on the Burnley Road site, into which reservoir the water gathered from this area will also be conveyed after filtration.

The present works consists of two storage reservoirs at Mitchell's House, with a capacity of about 188 million gallons, situated at a level of 977 OD., one reservoir at Dean Clough, Great Harwood, at an altitude of 530 OD., and with a capacity of about 224 million gallons, one service reservoir at Smalley Thorn, Great Harwood, of one million gallons capacity, situated at a level of 770 OD., and two service reservoirs at Burnley Road, Huncoat, at an altitude of 630 OD., with a joint capacity of 24 million gallons. In addition to these surface reservoirs, there is the underground supply at Altham, which, with the completion of the second scheme, it is hoped will realize from this station a supply equal to one million gallons per day.

The whole of the water from Dean Reservoir is filtered through open sand filters, this will apply also to the Mitchell's supply when the filters, now under reconstruction, are completed.

The present consumption is equal to about two and a quarter million gallons daily, and this is conveyed through over 85 miles of trunk mains. The number of consumers approximates 22,000, and the revenue income this year (1927-8) was £43,000.

GAS. Up to the year 1921, the gas required over the Board's area was manufactured at two works: one situated at Accrington, and the other at Great Harwood. The Accrington Works is now closed for manufacturing purposes and used only for storage.

The Board's Great Harwood Gas Works has been entirely re-modelled, and is capable of producing up to three million cubic feet of gas per diem.

The area was extended during 1923, so as to include the township of Whalley and part of the township of Billington.

The quantity of gas now produced per annum exceeds 610 million cubic feet, which is distributed through over 107 miles of trunk mains to upwards of 23,000 consumers, and nearly 2,000 public lamps. Approximately 140 tons of copper are taken from automatic meters yearly. The area supplied is roughly 25 square miles. For the year 1927, 31,530 tons of coal were distilled, and 173,689 gallons of petroleum used. The products were 200,000 cwts. of coke, 550,000 gallons of crude tar, and 530,800 lbs. of sulphate of ammonia. Gas was used through the following appliances, exclusive of lighting; Cookers, 13,200; Wash Boilers, 13,718; Grillers, etc., 9,000; Fires and Radiators, 1,455; Geysers, 177; Engines, 84; and Furnaces, 113. The revenue income of the Gas Department for 1927-8, exceeded £135,000.

FINANCE. The Gas and Water Undertakings were purchased by the Board as from the 1st January, 1895, the purchase price being £767,400; made up as follows:

	Gas. £	Water. £
To "A" and "B" and the 5 % Debenture Stock holders, Annuities, equal to maximum dividends of 10% and 8% respectively and the agreed interest capitalized value equals	326,900	420,000
Cash Payment	11,800	8,700
	£338,700	£428,700

Provision to redeem the above Annuities has to be made by 1955, and at 31st March, 1928, this had been done to the following extent:

Gas.	Water.
£126,295 6s. 1d.	£163,409 10s. 4d.

leaving the net indebtedness at that date on this account at
£200,604   13s.   11d.   £256,590   9s.   8d. respectively.

Since the incorporation of the Board, further capital has been raised for the two undertakings, as under:

	£
Gas	£308,127
Water	129,675

In redemption of these borrowings and the cash payments, there had accumulated to 31st March, 1928, the sums of £138,360 13s. 8d., and £77,284 15s. 10½d. respectively, leaving the total net indebtedness of the Board as under:

Gas	£382,171 0s. 3d.
Water	£317,680 13s. 9½d.

SEWERAGE AND SEWAGE DISPOSAL.

THE report of Benjamin Herschel Babbage, Esq., Superintending Inspector of the General Board of Health, dated May, 1850, gives much interesting information concerning the drainage and sewering of the town, then having an estimated population of about 11,000. "The town is very badly drained. Stone drains have been laid down most of the main streets, but they are of a very rude construction, being formed without mortar, and vary in sizes, inclinations, and forms, having been made at the expense of the different owners of property in their neighbourhood, a portion of drain at one time and a portion at another, the object of each person having been to remove the drainage as well as he could from his own premises without reference to his neighbours. The consequence of such an entire want of system is, as might naturally be expected, that these drains are generally very inefficient, requiring constant cleaning out, repairing and altering."

"This brook (Hyndburn), which runs throughout the length of the town, receives the drainage from all the ditches, surface drains, and sewers both in New and Old Accrington. Many of the privies open directly into this brook."

The outcome of this report was that a system of pipe sewers was laid down which, in a comparatively short period, proved entirely inadequate for the rapidly growing town.

This problem was very acute at the time of the Incorporation of the Borough, and in 1881, the Corporation requisitioned Messrs. Newton and Vauser, Civil Engineers, to devise an adequate system of main sewerage. The question of an outlet for the sewerage system was difficult, as there was no possible site available in the Borough. Many sites were suggested, and the choice centred between Martholme and Coppy Clough, the latter eventually being decided upon. This, in turn, raised the question of amalgamation with Church, which proposal was turned down by Parliament in 1882.

The Accrington Improvement Act, 1882, provided for the formation of a Joint Sewerage Board for Accrington and Church, and that the Local Government Board should settle the matter of the main sewerage outlet. After a three days' local inquiry, Coppy Clough was selected as the site, and the Accrington and Church Outfall Sewerage Board was formed in 1884. Mr. R. Sharples was appointed Clerk to the Board, which position he still holds. The Board proceeded with the construction of the Main Outfall sewers to link up with the sewers of the Borough and Church, and the first

Sewage Disposal Works was opened at Coppy Clough in May, 1889.

It is interesting to note that the Main Outfall sewer from near Church Bridge to Coppy Clough is 6 feet high and 4 feet 8 inches wide, and constructed in brickwork, being about 50 feet from the surface where it passes under the Canal.

The construction of the Main Sewers and Intercepting Sewers was continued, and the whole of the sewage of the present developed portion is now carried to Coppy Clough Works. The lines and design of these Main and Intercepting Sewers is such that to-day there is a complete absence of flooding in the Borough, a very different state of affairs to that in 1889, when a severe storm visited the town and caused much damage to property, especially at Woodnook and Blackburn Road near the Market, the streets being flooded to a depth of several feet.

The Main and Intercepting Sewers are principally brick egg-shaped culverts varying in size from 4 feet 9 inches by 4 feet to 3 feet by 2 feet. Some are circular, of diameters of 4 feet, 3 feet, and 2 feet. They are laid in Hyndburn Road, Union Street, Blackburn Road, Abbey Street, Plantation Street, Water Street, Cambridge Street, Burnley Road, Castle Street, Owen Street, Haywood Street, India Street, Lonsdale Street, Countess Street, Portland Street, Willows Lane, Brown Street, and Victoria Street. One of the most interesting is that in Haywood Street, which was constructed to take the drainage from the Dyke Nook District of Whalley Road, so situated as not to be in the Watershed draining to Coppy Clough. This was constructed by means of tunnelling from Owen Street along the line of the then intended Haywood Street to the point where this Street now named Haywood Road joins Livingstone Road at the Borough Boundary. At the point where it crosses Queen's Road, it is over 50 feet deep from the surface. The foresight displayed in the construction of this sewer, made it possible to utilise the Laneside Estate for Housing purposes. The development and sewering of building estates has also proceeded on sound lines during this period, so that the present sewerage system will be adequate for the future development which may be expected within the present boundaries of the Borough.

The original Outfall Works consisted of five large tanks, two of which were used as preliminary settling tanks, the sewage from these being drawn off after remaining quiescent for a short time, into one or other of the remaining tanks where it was allowed further time for settlement, the clarified or partially clarified sewage was then run off directly into the river; a small quantity of lime was added to precipitate the solid matters contained in the sewage. No method was adopted for filtration.

In 1895-96, the Works were partially re-modelled, when filters, contact beds, pressing plant, etc., were constructed to deal with the precipitated settled sewage. During the year 1897-98, experiments were conducted embracing various methods of sewage treatment and filtration on biological lines; the experiments were so successful that further extensions were carried out consisting of percolating bacteria beds having revolving distributors, humus tanks, etc., these beds were the first to be installed in this country.

Subsequently, the Royal Commission on Sewage Disposal was actively engaged making enquiries and collecting evidence as to the best available means of dealing with the sewage problem, and constant experiments were carried on at the Board's Works by and for the Royal Commission, valuable reports being issued from time to time.

In 1909, an additional 4½ acres of land adjacent to the Works was obtained, after arbitration as to price. Plans were prepared for completely re-modelling and extending the Works, which work was proceeding for some five years, at a cost of about £23,000. The Works now consist of a screening plant, sewage reception tank, storm water tank, septic tanks, 28 bacteria beds, and 14 humus tanks. The sewage, after passing the screen, is discharged through specially prepared openings into the sewage reception tank, where the heavier solids are deposited, and from thence through the septic tanks where the quality of the sewage is equalized and made more uniform in strength. The septic sewage is then drawn off and discharged by means of revolving arms, and percolates through the coke of the bacteria beds. The changes that take place in the beds may be classed as physical, chemical, and biological; the bacterial changes are those chiefly concerned in the conversion of ammonia to nitric acid, the process known as nitrification, and the subsequent oxidation of organic matter by means of the nitrate formed.

The effluent from the bacteria beds passes through a series of humus tanks which are 25 feet square, and 30 feet in depth. These tanks form an inverted pyramid, baffle plates are fixed at the entrance to each tank so that the effluent enters some 4 feet 6 inches below the surface instead of skimming the surface, the advantage being that the weight of water above helps to force the matter in suspension to the bottom of the tanks where an outlet pipe discharges the sludge to the sludge well. The effluent, after passing through the humus tanks, is finally discharged into the River Hyndburn.

Storm water is dealt with in a special tank, which tank becomes operative when the flow exceeds three times the dry weather flow. It is afterwards passed through a series of six humus tanks and thence discharged into the River.

The resulting sludge from the various tanks is discharged on to large under-drained lagoons, and when dry and spadeable it is taken by a motor driven truckway to the Sewerage Board's wharf adjoining the Leeds and Liverpool Canal, and taken away by boat for manurial purposes.

Up to the year 1914, steam was the principal motive power used at the Works, but by raising the septic tanks, the whole of the bacteria beds can now be operated by gravitation, and steam has been entirely dispensed with. Electric motors have been installed to work the air compressor, pumps, presses, truckway, etc. The motive power is obtained from a dynamo driven by a 40 B.H.P. water turbine supplied from the River Hyndburn. This dynamo supplies the several motors and the whole of the electric lighting of the works. The turbine not being sufficient to run the whole of the plant in very dry seasons, a supply of electricity is obtained from the mains of the Accrington Corporation as a standby. By dispensing with coal, the Board is saving at least three thousand pounds per annum.

Since the Works were re-modelled in 1914, they have been thoroughly efficient; the cost of sewage disposal to Accrington and Church only amounts to a rate of approximately 6d. in the £. The capacity of the Works is estimated to be sufficient for the requirements of Accrington and Church for many years to come. Such results reflect the skill and care which has been exercised in the construction and development of this important work for the community.

THE GEOLOGY OF ACCRINGTON AND DISTRICT.
by John Ranson, A.M.I.M.E., F.G.S.
Lecturer in Geology and Botany at the Municipal Technical College, Blackburn.

THE town of Accrington stands on the Lower Coal Measures, a formation consisting of shales, mudstones, sandstones, coal seams, and fireclay with gannister. These rocks attain a thickness of about 1,100 feet. They are overlain by a small thickness of Middle Coal Measures (on Moleside and Hameldon) whose base the Arley Mine which sweeps round the end of Moleside was the scene of remarkable activity during the coal strikes of 1921 and 1926, when outcrop workers with primitive appliances won the coal at considerable risk to life and limb.

The base of the Lower Coal Measure is taken at the six inch mine, below which lie the Millstone grits so called because they were used for millstones before the introduction of modern milling machinery. It is of interest to note that a pair of millstones may still be seen on Whalley Banks, apparently where they were quarried long ago.

STRATIGRAPHY.

The following table shews the various geological formations within easy walking distance of Accrington.

Period.	Formation.
Recent	Peat, Alluvium, River Gravels.
Glacial	Boulder Clay, Sands and Gravels.
Permo-Trias	Red and Yellow Sandstones. Unconformity.
Upper Carboniferous	Middle Coal Measures. Lower Coal Measures. Millstone Grits.

Lower Carboniferous   Pendleside Limestones.
Worston Shales.
Upper Carboniferous Limestone.
Lower Carboniferous Limestone.

GLACIAL PHENOMENA.

Evidences of ice work in the district are numerous and interesting. They are:
1. Glaciated, i.e., ice worn rocks.
2. Terminal curvature of rocks with high dip.
3. Glacial drift with erratics.

Glaciated rocks are well seen at Bold Venture Quarry, Chatburn, and Horrocksford Quarry, Clitheroe, especially during uncovering operations when the limestones are seen to be highly polished, grooved and striated, the striae running S. 30° W. at Chatburn thus indicating the direction of moving ice.

At Turn Hill in the Calder Gap at Whalley, the Millstone Grits have been well rounded, and striated by the ice which pushed through the gap. The striae are not so well shown as at Clitheroe.

Terminal Curvature is well displayed in many places along the Pendle range where the Millstone Grits, dipping at high angles, have had their outcropping portions forced over against the direction of dip as in the illustration at Rishton Quarries.

Slight downhill curvature might be due to "creep" but surface disturbances of this magnitude demand another cause.

Confirmation that this curvature is the result of ice-work is shown by the fact that in some places the rocks have been pushed over in an uphill as well as a downhill direction. This was well exemplified during the excavation of the puddle trench of the Parsonage Reservoir for Blackburn Corporation, the shales and interbedded grits were strongly turned over in an uphill direction, and the ice, passing over the hilltop, bent back the strata on the dip slope as in the illustration from Close Brow Quarry near Rishton.

TERMINAL CURVATURE IN HASLINGDEN FLAGS, CLOSE
BROW QUARRY, RISHTON.

GLACIAL DEPOSITS are represented by the well-known boulder clay and sands and gravels so widespread over the district. These deposits are naturally thickest on low ground and thin out on high hillsides.

Two types of glacial drift are recognizable in the district, viz., the North-Western Drift and Ribblesdale Drift. The former is due to Irish Sea ice advancing across the district and surmounting the lower hills and crossing the valleys, bringing with it abundant erratics from the Lake District and the Southern Uplands of Scotland. The lavas, ashes, and breccias of the Borrowdale Volcanic Series, Eskdale Granite and the Buttermere and Ennerdale Granophyre being especially representative of Lakeland erratics and the Criffel-Dalbeattie Granite, the most readily recognized type of erratic from Southern Scotland.

Lake District erratics are the most plentiful of foreign rocks in the drifts of the area and occur as far north as Clitheroe, and I have found occasional specimens even at Chatburn, and the Buttermere Granophyre on the sides of Pendleton Brook on Pendle Hill, at 550 feet.

Dr. A. Wilmore has shown me a large specimen of Riebeckite Eurite from Ailsa Craig, which he found on Longridge Fell during excavations for a reservoir there.

Shap Granite is said to have been discovered from time to time, but whenever specimens have been kept for verification they have usually been found to be the red variety of Eskdale Granite. I have only seen one boulder of Shap Granite in the Accrington district drift during many years of careful observation, and this was not typical of the main mass of that rock. Similarly, many of the erratics supposed to be Criffel Granite, have turned out to be the grey variety of Eskdale Granite.

Ribblesdale Drift is usually a stiff blue clay full of limestone boulders and chert from the limestones of the valley, together with carboniferous grits and sandstones and the characteristic Silurian Grit (Austwick Grit) of Upper Ribblesdale. A large boulder of the latter occurs on the shoulder of Pendle near little Mearley Clough, and smaller ones are very numerous all over this part of Ribblesdale.

Ribblesdale drift interdigitates with North-Western drift at Whalley as pointed out by Professor P. F. Kendall.

In the Calder Gap below Moreton Hall, the glacial conglomerate in the river and on its banks consists of Ribblesdale drift cemented by the partial solution of limestone boulders, while on the footpath to Whalley Banks, numerous Lakeland erratics may be seen. It seems clear, therefore, that the Ribblesdale ice was overpowered here by the North-Western ice and thrust through the Calder Gap which was obviously, therefore, already in existence.

The most remarkable Pennine erratic, however, is that of the Ingletonian Conglomerate and grit which occurs sporadically in the area. This rock is well exposed in Chapel-le-Dale above Ingleton, and also in Ribblesdale, about Horton, at the foot of Penyghent. It has the appearance of an igneous rock, and is very distinctive.

GLACIAL CONGLOMERATE IN RIVER CALDER.

The largest erratic of this rock weighing several tons, lies on Seat Naze, in Rossendale, at an elevation of 990 feet along with North-Western drift. The writer and Mr. J. Spencer, were the first accurately to identify it in 1912, and Dr. R. H. Rastall, of Cambridge, the Authority on the Ingletonian Series of Ingleton, confirmed this. *

A second large boulder was found at Red Pump, and presented to the writer by Mr. T. C. Stephenson, of Whalley. Others have been found at Bacup by Mr. James Hargreaves.

From the distribution of Ribblesdale drift it seems clear that the Ribblesdale Glacier split on the north end of the Pendle range, one branch going down the Burnley Valley, and the other down Ribblesdale for some distance.

GLACIAL SANDS AND GRAVELS are well developed in many parts of the district. They are usually seen to be much current-bedded and to contain streaks and patches of heavier materials often with numerous erratics of northern origin as may be seen in the Sand pits at Knuzden.

These deposits were produced by the melting of the ice-sheet and consequent sorting of liberated materials.

Lake Accrington, a glacial lake with a probable area of forty to fifty square miles, was formed during the retreat of the ice-sheet from this district. It appears to have been held up by a large ice-barrier and glacial deposits on the north-west, and apparently overflowed for a long time by way of the Cliviger Gorge to whose formation, therefore, it largely contributed before finding a lower outlet at Brinscall. For a fuller account of these interesting features, the reader is referred to the literature cited.

Another glacial overflow of later date was responsible for cutting the Hoghton Gorge, near Preston, now occupied by the River Darwen.

*R. H. Rastall. "The Ingletonian Series of West Yorkshire." Prae. Yorks. Geol. Soc. Vol. lxvi, 1906.

There had previously been a gap of appreciable size through this part of the Pendle range whose sides were as wide apart as Hoghton Cliff, and Cabin Hill at the end of Yellow Hills.

This gap was a pre-glacial one as proved by the drift covered grits on both sides of it. It extended through the Pleasington Golf Links where the glacial sands, about one hundred feet in thickness, block the old river gap, and incidentally, provide the finest golf course in the district.

PERMO-TRIAS.
Rocks of this age are but poorly represented in the district. A small patch occurs at Clitheroe, and is seen to rest unconformably on the limestones above Stephen Bridge at Bashall Brook.

Higher up Bashall Brook, red and yellow sandstone with quartzite pebbles of Bunter age overlies the Millstone Grits. These interesting relics are important as shewing the large amount of denudation which had taken place in pre-Permo-Triassic time.

Above Roach Bridge on the river Darwen, Permo-Trias rests unconformably on the Sabden Shales.

A microscopic examination of the sand grains of these rocks by the writer has revealed numerous well rounded grains obviously wind-blown, while among the heavy mineral constituents zircons were conspicuous as also were black coated grains.

LOCAL SECTIONS OF WELL EXPOSED STRATA.
Of the local sections of Lower Coal Measures which may be commended to the student of Stratigraphy, those exposed in Priestley, Shoe Mill, and Tom Dule's Clough, Warmden Clough, and Tag Clough, will be found most interesting and accessible, they shew 300 to 400 feet of the lower and most important part of the above measures.

The upper part of the series may be studied on the Coppice, and at Castle Clough, where a fine section occurs from just above the Pasture Mine to near the base of the Old Lawrence Rock, the latter being well exposed in the quarries above.

Various comparative vertical sections of strata passed through in local bore-holes will be found in the recently issued Mem. Geol. Surv., "The Geology of the Rossendale Anticline," (1927).

I wish to thank my friend Mr. N. Haworth, for the following section and for his unstinted assistance for many years, in the study of the local Coal Measures.

SECTION IN PRIESTLEY, SHOE MILL, AND TOM DULE'S CLOUGHS.

Thickness of Strata.		
Feet.	Inches	
90	0	Book-leaf Shales. In Tom Dule's Clough and Higher Antley Brick Works.
1	0	Cannel Coal. In Tom Dule's Clough and Higher Antley Brick Works.
4	0	Fireclay. In Tom Dule's Clough and Higher Antley Brick Works.
30	0	Icconhurst (Rock) Sandstone. Exposed below Icconhurst Farm.
1	6	Upper Mountain or 40 yards Mine, and one foot of bastard coal beneath at Accrington and above at Huncoat.
2	0	Fireclay.
42	0	Warmden Sandstone.
-	3	Inch Mine
2	0	Fireclay.
54	0	Shales. (Dewhurst Shales.)
1	0	Upper Foot Coal.
1	6	Fireclay.
27	0	Great Arc Sandstone.
27	0	Shales.
2	0	Lower Mountain Mine or Gannister Coal.
4	0	Fireclay with Gannister.

For a full account of Ice work in N.E. Lancashire, the student is referred to the excellent papers of R. H. Tiddeman. "On the Evidence for the Ice Sheet in North Lancashire." Q.J.G.S., Vol. XXVIII, 1872.
A. Iowett. "The Glacial Geology of East Lancashire." Q.J.G.S., Vol. LXX, 1914.
Geol. Survey Map, Sheet 76 (Drift), 1' to 1 mile, 1927.

The Lower Mountain Mine is exposed on the stream side (Woodnook Water) above Woodnook Mill and below the weir. At the weir is a reversed fault, not seen, but proved in the coal-workings. Here the thickness of the coal was doubled by the fault.

The coal is succeeded by 27 feet of Shales well seen along the stream to Rothwell Mill where they are followed by 27 feet of Sandstone the Great Arc Sandstone, which is ripple-marked in places, thus showing evidence of current action during deposition. In Shoe Mill Clough below Shoe Mill, the Upper Foot Coal occurs on the stream side and has been much worked by outcroppers during the coal strikes of recent years. The overlying Shales contain bullions with goniatites and pterinopecten.

The section is continued in the tributary stream from Tom Dule's Clough, Baxenden. The Upper Foot Coal is covered by the Dewhurst Shales which higher upstream are faulted against the Book-leaf Shales, the fault is visible where it crosses the stream by the lower of the two small waterfalls in which the Icconhurst Sandstone is exposed. Immediately above, the fireclay below the Cannel Coal forms a small waterfall but the coal is not now exposed.

Behind Baxenden Station, the Millstone Grits are brought in by the large boundary fault. In the old brickworks quarry now disused Rough Rock (first Grit) is seen resting on thick shales, and nearer the Station Haslingden Flags (second Grits) are exposed.

It is interesting to note that the Lower Mountain Mine and Upper Foot Coals unite to form the "Union Mine" at Hapton Valley Colliery, Deerplay Pit, near Bacup, and Bank Hall Colliery, Burnley, the resulting coal seam then attaining a thickness of about four feet.

The Upper Foot or Bullion Mine is a very persistent coal and is traceable over a wide area and into Yorkshire, where its equivalent is known as the Halifax Hard Bed. Next to its wide distribution, this seam is famous for the sporadic occurrence in it of coal-balls containing plant remains in a remarkably good state of preservation. In the shales above the coal, fossils are numerous, and bullions (calcareous concretions) occur with goniatites in great perfection, viz., Gastrioceras sub-crenatum (Carbonarium), Gastrioceras listeri, and Gastrioceras Coronatum with Pterinopecten papyraceus, and Posidonomya gibsoni, etc.

Another good section which may be studied in an evening's stroll is that in Warmden Clough.

The section begins in a tiny stream which enters Warmden Brook below the reservoir embankment. Here the gannister and fireclay below the Lower Mountain Mine are well exposed, the coal, however, is not now in evidence owing to the activity of outcroppers.

Above the position of the coal are shales capped with the Great Arc Sandstone. The latter is better seen at the waterfall and gorge immediately above Warm den Reservoir. This sandstone is followed by fireclay and the Upper Foot Coal at present exposed in trial holes on the right bank of the gorge.

Above the Great Arc Waterfall the Dewhurst Shales are exposed in the next part of the Clough, and higher up are capped by the lower part of the massive Warmden Sandstone which forms a steep cliff. At the junction of the Warmden Sandstone and the Dewhurst Shales the Inch Mine is to be seen showing three inches of coal and about two feet of fireclay. This is the thinnest coal seam in the district and curiously enough is very widespread and persistent throughout the area.

The upper part of the Warmden Sandstone is well seen in Warmden Quarry. This excellent stone has long been used for building, and for setts, kerbs, etc., owing to the high cost of uncovering and working it, however, the quarry has been abandoned. The upper part of this sandstone is false-bedded and contains numerous balllike concretions.

The Warmden Sandstone is succeeded elsewhere in the district by the Upper Mountain Mine (or 40 Yards Mine), this coal seam is absent in the Warmden area although there is cover enough for it.

The Warmden Sandstone is also exposed in a small quarry on the side of Priestley Clough.

GREAT ARC SANDSTONE, WARMDEN CLOUGH.

At Higher Antley Brickworks Quarry the Book-leaf shales are seen to rest on the Cannel Coal and its fireclay bed.

The Cannel Coal is at present visible in a number of outcrop workings on the stream bank in the upper part of Tag Clough where it is overlain by the Book-leaf shales and the Flag and Slate Rock or Crutchman Sandstone, higher up stream. The latter rock, a thinly bedded micaceous flag and tile stone, was formerly much worked at the Crutchman Quarry at Warmden, where, owing to the presence of a couple of faults the rocks have been thrown down for 40 yards on the Warmden Quarry side and 30 yards on the road side opposite, with the result that their normal approximate horizontality has been disturbed and they are seen to dip at angles from 10° to 40°.

A trace of the Pasture Mine was to be seen on top of the Crutchman Sandstone but is no longer visible.

The Crutchman Sandstone was also quarried at Green Haworth, and the deserted workings now make an efficient bunker on the Golf Course.

Above the Pasture Mine lie the Accrington Mudstones of great economic value. These mudstones, 120 feet in thickness, are well exposed at Whinney Hill Quarry, and on the Coppice where they are also quarried for brick making, for which purpose there is no better material in the country.

The Accrington Mudstones are capped by the Old Lawrence Rock, a sandstone which has been quarried in many places on the Coppice. The great quarries on Hameldon Scout, whose spoil banks stand out so boldly on Burnley Road, are also in this rock. The Old Lawrence Rock is followed by shales and ragstones, and these are covered by the Riddle Scout Rock, a sandstone some fifty feet in thickness, then come more shales and the Arley Mine, the base of the Middle Coal Measures.

From the Arley Mine to the Flag and Slate Rock or Crutchman Sandstone, the measures are about seven hundred feet thick; the remaining four hundred feet below contain the measures of most interest and economic value, they are, moreover, better displayed around the district.

This brief account of the coal measures of Accrington with their stratigraphic, scenic, and economic interest, is but an introduction to the geology of a larger area within easy walking distance of the town. The Coal Measures are the uppermost and smallest series of the Carboniferous rocks of the district, beneath them lie the massive Millstone Grit Series of the Pendle Range and the Carboniferous Limestones of Clitheroe and Ribblesdale whose base is not seen locally. Since Whalley Banks, Pendle Hill, and the Ribble Valley form the happy hunting ground of a large and ever increasing number of our citizens, it may not be out of place to give such an account of their geology as will enable them to appreciate the wonders of these delightful places and the causes to which they are due.

THE MILLSTONE GRIT SERIES.

The use of goniatites as indices of geological horizons in this district during the last few years, has made it possible to classify the Millstone Grit Series with greater precision than was possible hitherto.

One outstanding result of importance emerged, viz., that the Kinderscout Grit, formerly regarded as underlying the Sabden Shales, was proved to overlie them.

Lithologically, the grits range from fine sandstones to quartzose grits and conglomerate. Their materials are such as would be provided by an upland region of granitic rocks, etc. Messrs. L. H. Tonks and W. B. Wright, have observed that the series thickens when traced in a south-westerly direction in this part of Lancashire.

THE INFLUENCE OF THE MILLSTONE GRITS ON LOCAL SCENERY.

It will be noted from the preceding table that the Millstone Grits are divided into an upper and lower series by the Sabden Shales, some 1,500 to 2,000 feet thick.

These grits and shales illustrate admirably the "Law of Structures," viz., that hard rocks tend to stand out in strong relief while the softer rocks form the lower ground.

Nowhere is this better exemplified than along the Pendle Range, a twin range of hills composed of the thick masses of upper and lower grits separated by the Sabden Shales.

MILLSTONES IN LOWER MILLSTONE GRITS, WHALLEY BANKS.

The ridge running from Blacko via Padiham Heights, Black Hill, Rishton Quarries, Revidge, Blackburn Park, and Billinge Hill to Hoghton Cliff, is composed of the various members of the Upper Grits, the Revidge and Kinderscout Grits exerting a predominating influence along the hill tops. While the parallel ridge to this running from Pendle Summit via Clerk Hill, Whalley Banks and Wilpshire to Mellor Beacon is composed of the Pendle or Wilpshire Grits.

The Sabden Shales being soft rocks have been easily washed out along their strike to form the intervening valleys as seen at Pendle Water, (Rough lee) Sabden Valley, Dean Valley, and along Knotts Brook.

The same principle is illustrated on the face of Pendle Hill above Clitheroe and Whalley. Here the lower Pendle Grit makes the crest of the hill and the Bowland Shales the steep hillside. The characteristic curve so produced will be noted repeatedly when traversing the Bowland fells.

In the Bowland Shales is an impersistent grit the Pendleside Grit, which quickly passes laterally into shales. When present, this grit often forms small waterfalls in the streams as in Little Mearley Clough on Pendle Hill.

THE LOWER CARBONIFEROUS SERIES.
It is not an easy matter to state where the line should be drawn between the Upper and Lower Carboniferous Rocks. I have previously taken it at the base of the Bowland Shales on lithological grounds. Mr. Bisat, however, makes the separation about the middle of the Bowland Shales where an apparent palaeontological break occurs and the genus goniatites (sensu stricto) appears for the last time and the genus Eumorphoceras makes its first appearance. There does not appear to be a stratigraphical break in this district corresponding to the one in the South-Western Province.

The Pendleside Limestones are dark cherty limestones which with interbedded shales attain a thickness of about 600 feet. They make a marked shoulder on the side of Pendle Hill and are cut through by several streams which have thereby formed striking cloughs and gullies.

Beneath them are the Worston Shales which constitute the main part of the old "Shales with Limestones." These shales are dark argillaceous and unfossiliferous and about 1,200 feet thick: they make the low ground between the foot of Pendle and the knoll limestones.

Rising from the low ground are the well-known knolls of Worsaw, Salt Hill, Gerna, and Twiston, etc. These knolls are composed of the massive white fossiliferous Upper Carboniferous Limestone of S. age. Their peculiar character is ascribed to the mode of accumulation of their limestones (900 to 1,400 feet thick) and subsequent dissection.

Further out in the valley is a second line of knolls typified by Coplow, Knunck Knowles, and Waddow, etc.

At Coplow, over 400 feet of limestones are displayed mainly white and massive with subordinate bedded limestones and thin shales. Fossils again are very numerous and characteristic of C zone. The lowest limestones of the series are known as the Chatburn Limestones from the place where they are typically developed. They show a thickness of about 700 feet, but their base is not seen. Since their age ranges from Z to C1, it is very probable that the older palaeozoic floor underlies these limestones at no great depth.

In contrast to the knoll limestones of the Coplow and Salt Hill Series, the Chatburn Limestones are dark well-bedded rocks with shale partings. They are not very fossiliferous. Good exposures of them may be seen about Chatburn, especially at Bold Venture Quarry and in the railway cutting north of Chatburn Station, also at the Horrocksford or Lane End Quarry near Clitheroe, and the Bankfield Quarries.

For a full account of these interesting rocks, the student is referred to Dr. Parkinson's excellent paper with a full bibliography.

TECTONICS.
If a geological map of the area briefly described, is consulted, it will be seen that the rocks trend generally N.E.-S.W. to E.N.E.-W.S.W., and are arranged along the axes of a couple of great folds, viz., the Burnley-Blackburn Syncline a great trough-like fold in which the coal-measures are preserved and the Clitheroe Anticline, a huge archlike fold which has been dissected almost to the base of the limestones.

These structures were impressed on the district in late Carboniferous and early Permian time and are of considerable interest because the trend of their axes is different from those of the major folds of the same age elsewhere in the country.

The Pennine axis runs north and south; the Armorican axes east and west, while the local folds known as the Lancastrian flexures trend roughly N.E.-S.W., thus coinciding generally with the trend of the Caledonian folds of the older palaeozoic rocks to the north and doubtless continued beneath this district.

In addition to the Burnley-Blackburn Syncline, it is of interest to local geologists to note the occurrence of a low, flattened Anticline which runs from Grimshaw Park, Blackburn, via Stanhill, Church, Milnshaw, and Accrington Cemetery, where it is truncated by a large fault.

FAULTS.
Faults are very numerous in the area, their dominant trend being north-west to south-east. In addition to these, a series of east and west faults run through Accrington. Collectively, these faults have been responsible for much broken ground in the area which has occasioned considerable trouble to the miner.

GEOLOGY AND LOCAL INDUSTRY.
The principal coal seams, viz., the Upper and Lower Mountain Mines, have long been exploited and found employment for a large body of miners, the former, however, is almost worked out in Accrington township, and the latter fast approaches exhaustion locally, though considerable reserves are still available at Altham and Huncoat districts.

Formerly there was much quarrying in the district as the number of derelict quarries testifies, notably at Warmden Quarry where the Warmden sandstone was worked for building stone, setts, and kerbs, etc., until the cost of uncovering fresh rock caused working to be unremunerative. Nearby is the Crutchman Quarry where the thinly bedded Flag and Slate rock was once worked for flags, and tile-stones for roofing purposes before the introduction of true slates.

The great quarries along Hapton Scout in the Old Lawrence Sandstone and their huge spoil banks like mountain screes above Burnley Road, bear eloquent testimony to a once vigorous industry.

In contrast to the local decay of coal mining and quarrying, it is pleasing to note that brick making still flourishes at Whinney Hill, Enfield, and Huncoat, where the huge quarries at Whinney Hill and the Coppice afford evidence of man as a geological agent. The Accrington Mudstones worked there, make bricks second to none, hence the great demand for them from various parts of the country, and even farther afield.

GEOLOGY AND WATER SUPPLY.
With the rapid advance of industry and consequent growth of the town, it became imperative that an adequate water supply should be assured, and since all available surface supplies had already been secured it was necessary to bore into mother earth to recover the water which had filtered through the surface rocks. Fortunately, the geological structure of the district at Altham being that of a basin, some five or six square miles in area, readily lent itself to this venture. A bore-hole was sunk to a depth of 174 feet and a good supply of potable water obtained which, though rather hard at present, will probably improve in this respect in time to come.

So satisfactory and dependable has this new supply been, that steps are being taken to obtain a larger quantity by means of a deeper boring. It is believed that the water from this deeper boring will have a lower degree of hardness than that from the older source.

THE SCENERY OF ACCRINGTON DISTRICT.
Accrington is pleasantly situated among a ring of encircling hills which give it shelter and at the same time help to precipitate the rainfall and give rise to the numerous streams which course down the hillsides and through the local Cloughs. These Cloughs, on the whole, occupy pre-glacial hollows as shown by their drift covered sides, the streams, however, have cut down through the deposits of glacial drift and eaten into the native rocks with the result that where sandstones overlying shales have been encountered, charming waterfalls have been formed as a result of the superior durability of the sandstone. This is well seen in Warmden Clough at the fall known as the Great Arc, where a little gorge has been cut through the Great Arc Sandstone by the recession of the waterfall face.

Another example of this is seen in Cocker Brook where the Warmden Sandstone overlying the Dewhurst Shales gives rise to Cockerlumb fall, which is a pleasing sight in winter or summer.

— CENTRE OF

NORTH.
MELBOURNE STREET
Tannery
WHALLEY ROAD
MOORE STREET
DOWRY STREET
MARY ANN ST
CASTLE STREET
Brass Foundry
Market Hall
MARKET PLACE
Spring Mill (Cotton)
250
River Hyndburn
UNION STREET
CRAWSHAW STREET
SCHOOL ST
Drill Hall
EDGAR STREET
WILLOW STREET
Bowling Green
BRIDGE STREET
DAVY ST
QUEEN ST
TANNER ST
MILL STREET
—SCALE OF YARDS:—

ACCRINGTON 1928:—

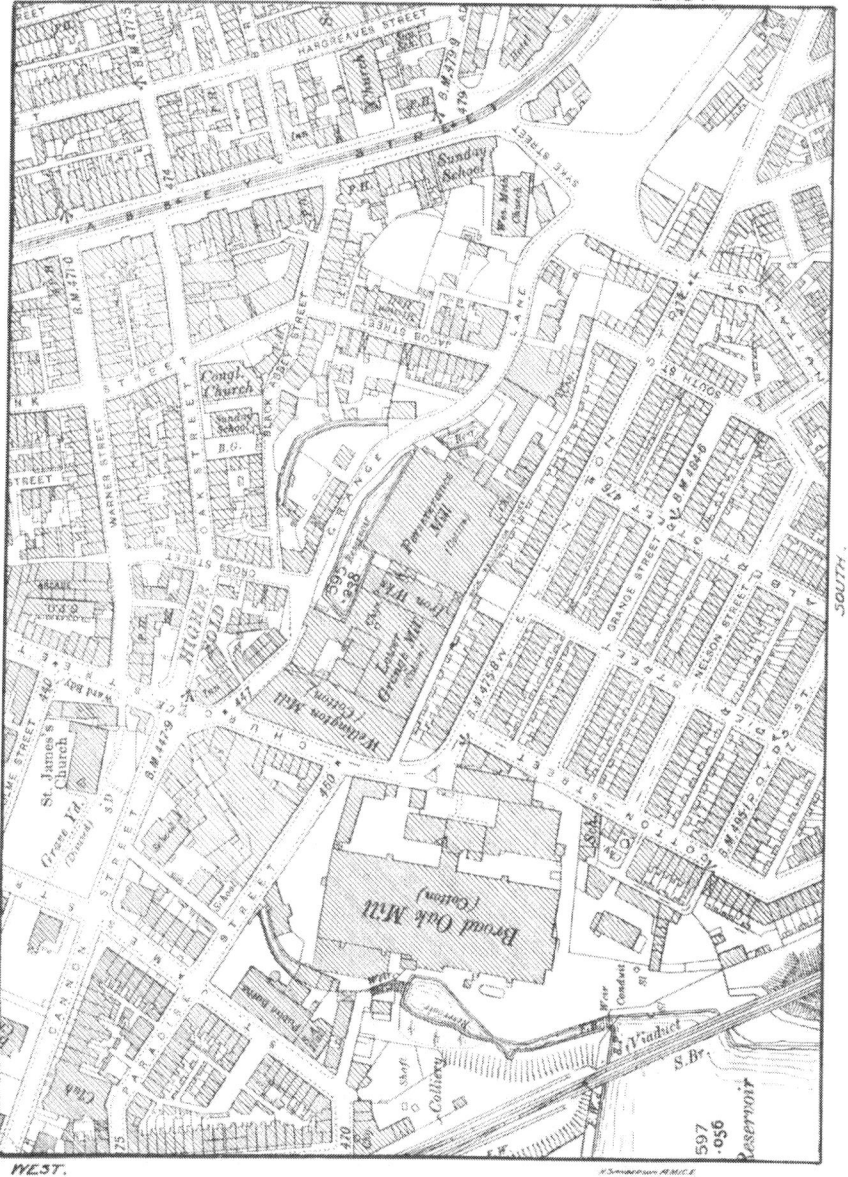

SOME SOCIAL AND NATIONAL EVENTS OF THE FIFTY YEARS.

IT is not the purpose of this Souvenir to do more than outline the corporate progress of the community, but social and national events of moment are so closely linked with the municipal life of the town that a brief outline of the main ones may be looked for.

THE VICTORIA HOSPITAL.

The period of the Incorporation was clouded by the strike in the Cotton Trade, which lasted from April 17th to June 18th, 1878: it also ends with the staple industry of Lancashire again under a cloud, which it is devoutly hoped will quickly be lifted. Other strikes have, unfortunately, marred the harmony of the community as, for example, the great coal strike of 1912, the prolonged dispute at Howard and Bullough's, commencing in 1914, and the last great social upheaval, the memory of which is still green, the National Railway strike of 1926. Disaster, also, overtook the district, and brought suffering to many homes on the 7th November, 1883, when an explosion occurred at the Colliery at Whinney Hill, sixty-eight persons being killed, and thirty injured.

War, too, is writ large upon the pages of our Jubilee History, such that all will hope may not mar the record of our town and land from now onwards. Not only the Great War of 1914-18, but the Boer War of 1899-1902. The opening of the Ambulance Drill Hall, by Major-General Baden-Powell, on June 11th, 1904, followed upon the close of the Boer War.

National events have been duly honoured the Jubilee and Diamond Jubilee of Queen Victoria, the Coronation of King Edward VII, and of our present King, and the visit of King George V and Queen Mary to the Borough, on the 9th July, 1913. These events were not allowed to pass without suitable commemoration.

An event of outstanding importance was the founding of the Victoria Hospital.

It was when Alderman Haywood was Mayor (in 1894) that a movement was made towards the establishment of a Hospital for Accrington and district. Prior to the opening of the Victoria Cottage Hospital, cases had been treated at the Blackburn Royal Infirmary and, in earlier days still, at Manchester. A meeting was held in the Town Hall, on January 25th, 1894, which was attended by 40 to 50 gentlemen of the district, and a Committee was appointed to carry out the unanimous desire of the meeting that a Hospital should be established in the town. The Mayor was appointed Hon. Treasurer, and Mr. A. H. Aitken, Town Clerk, Hon. Secretary. Part of the present site was secured, the appeal for subscriptions was generously responded to, and the first building with accommodation for 16 beds, opened on February 28th, 1898, by the then Mayor (Alderman Lee). The cost was a little over £7,000. Since that date many important additions, not only in structure but in apparatus, have been made. The first building extensions occurred in 1907, during the presidency of the then Mayor (Councillor Higham), when additional land was secured and the Hospital enlarged to accommodate 37 beds and 13 cots, with an immediate equipment of 33 beds and 12 cots, also a new administrative department. This provision, although generously contributed to by the public, left the Institution with a debt which was not finally cleared off until 1916.

In 1918, four additional beds and one more cot were added, making a total of 50 beds the extent of the present accommodation 38 for adults and 12 cots for children. It was during this year that improvements were also made to the Operating Theatre.

SOUP KITCHEN, INFANT STREET SCHOOL, 1895.

In 1927, the erection of a Nurses' Home adjacent to the Hospital was proceeded with, which building is now nearing completion. Its erection has been made possible by the contributions of the public to the Hospital Extensions Fund, an appeal for which was issued by the Committee of Management in 1925, resulting in a sum of upwards of £10,000 being raised up to the end of 1927. This amount has been supplemented this year by £5,144 11s. 9d., raised in connection with the efforts of Alderman Wilkinson during his Mayoralty, bringing the total to a sum which is expected to enable the Committee to open the Home free from debt. At the end of 1927, the Endowment Fund stood at £39,959 5s. 7d.

In accordance with the rules of the Hospital, the Mayor, during his term of office, is President for the time being, and the Hospital has been fortunate in having had at all times the active co-operation of each successive Mayor.

Distress and necessity have always brought forth in our townspeople a praiseworthy desire to render assistance. Not only was this evident in the great national conflicts of the period, but in very many more local cases too. In the early part of 1895, there was a long period of severe frost, with its attendant hardship for outdoor workers. A Soup Kitchen was established at Infant Street School, which is here illustrated. Many well-known Accringtonians of that day may be discovered in the group.

THE NEW POST OFFICE, 1922.

The Town's Improvements are dealt with elsewhere these are noticeable, not only in the main thoroughfares, but in public buildings also. Reference has already been made to the early days of the Post Office. This was moved in October, 1880, to Church Street, and continued there until 1922, when the new building in Abbey Street was opened.

Such, briefly, are the main social events of the fifty years. Those who have perused these pages will realize how great and rapid have been the strides made by the town during the past century. Others will pen the record of its progress during the next fifty years, and it will be nothing but creditable if the coming rulers realize, as those of the past have done, the inspiration of the Town's motto:

INDUSTRY AND PRUDENCE CONQUER.

MAYORS OF THE BOROUGH, 1878-1928.

1878-79;	1879-80.	John Emanuel Lightfoot.	1904-05;	1905-06.	Wm. Horrocks Rawson.
1880-81;	1881-82.	James Barlow.	1906-07;	1907-08.	T. E. Higham.
1882-83.		John Emanuel Lightfoot.	1908-09.		J. C. Lupton.
1883-84;	1884-85;	William Smith.	1909-10.		T. E. Nuttall.
1885-86.		William Entwisle.	1910-11;	1911-12.	A. S. Bury.
1886-87;	1887-88.	Thomas Hindle.	1912-13;	1913-14;	
1888-89;	1889-90.	Thomas Whittaker.	1914-15.		John Harwood.
1890-91;	1891-92; 1892-93.		1915-16. 1916-17.		John Barlow. James Henry Lupton.
1893-94;	1894-95.	Frederick N. Haywood.	1917-18;	1918-19	Doctor Counsell Dewhurst.
1895-96;	1896-97; 1897-98.	Williamson Lee.	1919-20.		David Walton Moffitt.
1898-99;	1899-1900	John S. Higham.	1920-21;	1921-22.	James Waddington.
1900-01.		D. L. Sprake.	1922-23.		Edward Woolley.
1901-02.		James Cunliffe.	1923-24;	1924-25.	Frederick Lord.
1902-03.		Thomas Broughton.	1925-26;	1926-27.	Charles Wilkinson.
1903-04.		John Duckworth.	1927-28.		T. E. Higham.

MEMBERS OF THE TOWN COUNCIL IN OFFICE IN THE JUBILEE YEAR.

The Mayor, Alderman Higham (1901).
Alderman Barlow (1908).
Alderman Bury (1901).
Alderman Ellis (1919).
Alderman Rawson (1891).
Alderman Sudall (1914).
Alderman Waddington (1898).
Alderman Wilkinson (1914).
Councillor Barlow (1923).
Councillor Baron (1926).
Councillor Beaton (1922).
Councillor Constantine (1919).
Councillor Harbinson (1923).
Councillor Higham (1928).
Councillor Lambert (1919).
Councillor Laytham (1925).

Councillor Livesey (1924).
Councillor Lord (1919).
Councillor O'Connor (1919).
Councillor Priestley (1928).
Councillor Roberts (1921).
Councillor Robinson (1925).
Councillor Slack (1920).
Councillor Snell (1919).
Councillor Sutcliffe (1923).
Councillor Tasker (1922).
Councillor Wade (1921).
Councillor Watson (1907).
Councillor J. Whittaker (1922).
Councillor W. Whittaker (1927).
Councillor Wilkinson (1915).
Councillor Woolley (1927).

Note. The date in brackets indicates the first year of election to the Council.

MISCELLANEA.

Area of the Borough, 3,427 acres.

Population (Census returns, 1851-1921).

1851............... 10,374	1891............... 38,602
1861............... 17,688	1901...............43,122
1871............... 21,788	1911............... 45,029
1881............... 31,435	1921............... 43,610

Number of Local Government Electors, 20,682.

Number of Parliamentary Electors in the Municipal Borough, 24,242.

LOCAL ACTS. The principal Acts of Parliament relating to the Borough are:

The Accrington Corporation Tramways Act, 1882	45 & 46 Vict. c. 118.
The Accrington Improvement Act, 1882	45 & 46 Vict. c. 173.
The Accrington Corporation Stearn Tramways (Haslingden and Rawtenstall Extension) Act, 1887	50 & 51 Vict. c. 56.
The Accrington Corporation (Consolidation of Loans) Act, 1890	53 & 54 Vict. c. 63.
The Accrington Corporation Act, 1905	5 Edw. 7 c. 43.

BIBLIOGRAPHY.

Ainsworth, Richard. Old Homesteads of Accrington and district (and many articles).
Baines, Edward. History of Lancashire.
Broughton, James. Accrington past and present. (Shopping Festival Souvenir, 1910.)
Burgess, W. H. Accrington and District Historical Notes. Printed in "Observer and Times," 1905.
Coucher Book of Kirkstall Abbey. (Thoresby Society.)
Court Rolls of the Manor of Clitheroe (Vol. III).
Crossley, R. S. Accrington, 100 years ago.
Crossley, R. S. Captains of Industry.
Crossley, R. S. Chronological Notes.
Domesday Book: Section relating to Lancashire and Cheshire.
Dugdale, Wm Monasticon Anglicanum.
Hargreaves, Benj. Recollections of Broad Oak.
*Nuttall, T. E. Occurrence of Palceoliths in N.E. Lancashire.
Victoria County History of Lancashire (Vols. VI and VII).
Whitaker, Thos. D. History of Whalley.
Williams, Rev. Chas. Accrington: A sketch of its history, 1872.
Williams, Rev. Chas. Accrington Mechanics' Institution: Story of 50 years. (1845 1895).

*Article in the Proceedings of the Prehistoric Society of East Anglia, Vol. II. With the exception of this item these books may be consulted at the Public Library.

Other books available

Darwen in its Hey Day
by L. Anne Hull

This fascinating book tells of the life and history of Darwen from the 1890s all the way through to World War I. The period was a great time of prosperity and growth for the town in which the population boomed and its iconic Tower was opened to the public.
An outstanding read by a local author.

Available for only £19.99 plus free p&p.

Bygone Blackburn
by Geo. C. Miller

This commemorative edition of Bygone Blackburn reveals the town's people and places of generations past. With stories revealing: The windmill at Eanam, the market cross and the stocks that were at the very hub of the town, poverty and riots that engulfed Blackburn in the 19th century plus much more.
Available for only £14.99.

Call 01254 245709
or visit our website:
www.HeritagePublications.co.uk

The perfect Christmas gift!
Blackburn:
in their own words

A fascinating collection of interviews with people living in and around Blackburn. Stories of the town that they grew up in. From struggles in times of worldwar, to happier times and prosperity.
Recorded in...
THEIR OWN WORDS.

Now available for only £12.99

Buy now from
01254 245709

Also available at: Lesley's News & Books on Blackburn Market

Blackburn Central Library

www.heritagepublications.co.uk

Printed in Poland
by Amazon Fulfillment
Poland Sp. z o.o., Wrocław